O9-BUB-286

FULLY DEVOTED

living
each day
in Jesus'
name

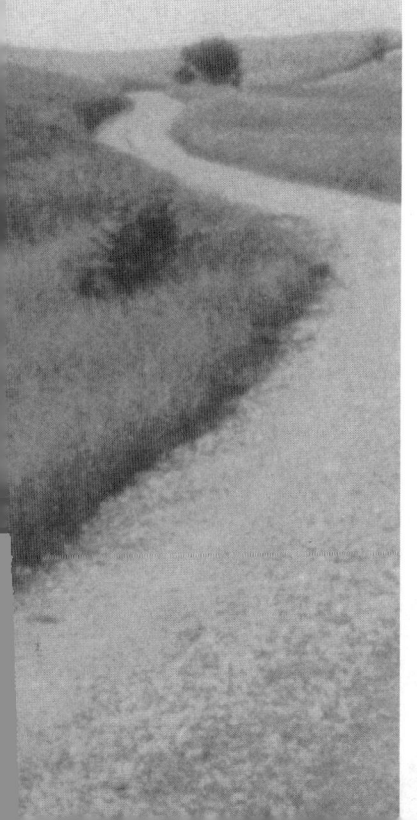

FULLY DEVOTED

living each day in Jesus' name

JOHN ORTBERG,
LAURIE PEDERSON,
JUDSON POLING

PURSUING SPIRITUAL TRANSFORMATION

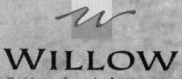

WILLOW
Willow Creek Resources

ZONDERVAN™

GRAND RAPIDS, MICHIGAN 49530 USA

WWW.ZONDERVAN.COM

We want to hear from you. Please send your comments about this book to us in care of the address below. Thank you.

GRAND RAPIDS, MICHIGAN 49530

w w w . z o n d e r v a n . c o m

ZONDERVAN™

Fully Devoted: Living Each Day in Jesus' Name
Copyright © 2000 by the Willow Creek Association

Requests for information should be addressed to:

Zondervan, *Grand Rapids, Michigan 49530*

ISBN 0-310-22073-4

All Scripture quotations unless otherwise noted are taken from the *Holy Bible: New International Version*®. NIV®. Copyright © 1973, 1978, 1984 by International Bible Society. Used by permission of Zondervan. All rights reserved.

All rights reserved. No part of this publication may be reproduced, stored in a retrieval system, or transmitted in any form or by any means—electronic, mechanical, photocopy, recording, or any other—except for brief quotations in printed reviews, without the prior permission of the publisher.

We are grateful for permission given by a number of gifted teachers to use excerpts from their books and messages for the opening readings in the sessions. These authors and speakers are acknowledged throughout this guide.

Interior design by Laura Klynstra Blost

Printed in the United States of America

10 11 12 13 14 15 /❖ EP/ 43 42 41 40 39 38 37 36 35 34 33

CONTENTS

Pursuing Spiritual Transformation

The Pursuing Spiritual Transformation series is all about being spiritual. But that may not mean what you think!

Do you consider yourself a spiritual person? What does that mean? Does spiritual growth seem like an impossible amount of work? Do you have a clear picture of the kind of life you'd live if you were to be more spiritual?

Each guide in the Pursuing Spiritual Transformation series is dedicated to one thing — helping you pursue authentic spiritual transformation. Here, in this introductory study, the goal is to help you define spiritual life and then live it as Jesus would live it.

You may find this study different from others you have done in the past. Each week in preparation for your group meeting, you will be completing a Bible study and experimenting with a variety of spiritual exercises. These elements are designed to enhance your private times with God and, in turn, to help you invite him into all aspects of your life, even the everyday routines. After all, spiritual life is just *life* — the one you live moment by moment.

It is very important that you complete this work before going to each meeting because the discussion is based on what you've learned from the study and what you've observed as a result of the spiritual exercise. The Bible study and exercises are not meant to be done an hour before the meeting, quickly filling in the blanks. Instead, we suggest you thoughtfully and prayerfully complete them over the course of several days as part of your regular devotional time with God.

A good modern Bible translation, such as the New International Version, the New American Standard Bible, or the New Revised Standard Version, will give you the most help in your study. You might also consider keeping a Bible dictionary handy to look up unfamiliar words, names, or places. Write your responses in the spaces provided in the study guide or use your personal journal if you need more space. This will help you participate more fully in the discussion, and will also help you personalize what you are learning.

When your group meets, be willing to join in the discussion. The leader of the group will not be lecturing but will encourage people to discuss what they have learned from the study and exercise. Plan to share what God has taught you. Try to be sensitive to the other members of the group. Listen attentively when they speak, and be affirming whenever you can. This will encourage more hesitant members of the group to participate. Be careful not to dominate the discussion. By all means participate, but allow others to have equal time. If you are a group leader or a participant who wants further insights, you will find additional comments in the Leader's Guide at the back of the study.

We believe that your ongoing journey through this material will place you on an exciting path of spiritual adventure. Through your individual study time and group discussions, we trust you will enter into a fresh concept of spiritual life that will delight the heart of God . . . and your heart too!

Ten Core Values
for Spiritual Formation

Spiritual transformation . . .

> . . . is essential, not optional, for Christ-followers.

> . . . is a process, not an event.

> . . . is God's work, but requires my participation.

> . . . involves those practices, experiences, and relationships that help me live intimately with Christ and walk as if he were in my place.

> . . . is not a compartmentalized pursuit. God is not interested in my spiritual life; he's interested in my *life*—all of it.

> . . . can happen in every moment. It is not restricted to certain times or practices.

> . . . is not individualistic, but takes place in community and finds expression in serving others.

> . . . is not impeded by a person's background, temperament, life situation, or season of life. It is available right now to all who desire it.

> . . . and the means of pursuing it, will vary from one individual to another. Fully devoted followers are handcrafted, not mass-produced.

> . . . is ultimately gauged by an increased capacity to love God and people. Superficial or external checklists cannot measure it.

Fully Devoted: Living Each Day in Jesus' Name

Years ago, a television commercial for an antacid asked, "How do you spell relief?" Their hope was that you'd spell it the same way they spelled their product name.

God asks us a similar question. He wonders, "How do you spell spirituality?" Naturally, he desires you to have the same perspective he does. Whatever words or phrases you come up with will define the path you walk and the goals you seek in your relationship with him. Answer that question well and you will be a fruitful follower of Christ. Answer it poorly and you will spend wasted years in pursuit of useless—even harmful—activities.

The goal of the Pursuing Spiritual Transformation series is simply this: to help you carefully define and then joyfully pursue spiritual life with God. This book is the first in that series. It introduces you to what we call "The Five Gs"—a framework which embraces five key areas of the Christian life. It is our hope that this tool will work like a good doctor—helping diagnose your spiritual condition and then prescribing the practices, experiences, and relationships you need to make progress. In this book, you'll learn what those Five Gs are. In subsequent studies you will explore one "G" per guide. You do not need to do the other books in any particular order, but we do recommend you do this book first to lay a foundation.

In doing this study—and the whole series—you may find that "being spiritual" is not what you thought. The good news is that the reality offered by God is so much better than the misconceptions. And it's readily available for you today.

SESSION ONE

WHAT IS
TRUE SPIRITUALITY?

What Is True Spirituality?

Reading by John Ortberg

Let's call him Hank. He had attended church since he was a boy, and now he was in his sixties. He was known by everyone—but no one really knew him. He had difficulty loving his wife. His children could not speak freely with him and felt no affection from him. He was not concerned for the poor, had little tolerance for those outside the church, and tended to judge harshly those who were inside.

One day an elder in the church asked him, "Hank, are you happy?"

Without smiling, he responded, "Yes."

"Well, then," replied the elder, "tell your face."

Hank's outside demeanor mirrored a deeper and much more tragic reality: *Hank was not changing.* He was not being transformed. But here's what is most remarkable: Nobody in the church was surprised by this. No one called an emergency meeting of the board of elders to consider this strange case of a person who wasn't changing. No one really expected Hank to change, so no one was surprised when it didn't happen.

There were *other* expectations in the church. People expected that Hank would attend services, would read the Bible, would affirm the right beliefs, would give money and do church work.

But people did not expect that day by day, month by month, decade by decade, Hank would be more transformed into the likeness of Jesus. People did not expect

No one really expected Hank to change, so no one was surprised when it didn't happen.

he would become a progressively more loving, joyful, winsome person. So they were not shocked when it did not happen.

How Is Spirituality Wrongly Understood?

> *How many people are radically and permanently repelled from The Way by Christians who are unfeeling, stiff, unapproachable, boringly lifeless, obsessive, and dissatisfied? Yet such Christians are everywhere, and what they are missing is the wholesome liveliness springing from a balanced vitality within the freedom of God's loving rule. ... "Spirituality" wrongly understood or pursued is a major source of human misery and rebellion against God.*
>
> —Dallas Willard, *The Spirit of the Disciplines*

"Spirituality" wrongly understood or pursued is a major source of human misery and rebellion against God.

Think of the irony: spiritual life leading to lifelessness. Spiritual growth producing misery. A life supposedly yielded to God rebelling against him! Obviously it's not supposed to be this way, yet for many, it's the sad truth.

When people are not being authentically transformed—when they are not becoming more loving, joyful, Christlike persons—they often settle for what might be called "pseudo-transformation."

We know that somehow we are supposed to be different than those outside the church. But if our heart isn't changing, we will look for more superficial and visible ways of demonstrating that we are "spiritual." We might:

- think spiritual maturity is simply about how much biblical or theological information we have acquired;
- think we should rigidly immerse ourselves in a host of spiritual practices or disciplines that will prove how spiritual we are;
- find ourselves looking down on people who are not working at their spiritual lives as hard as we are—so all of our efforts end up making us more judgmental and competitive rather than more loving; or

- focus solely on outward behaviors, making them the litmus test of godliness, while ignoring deeper — and more destructive — sins of the heart.

We need only to hear Jesus' words to the religious leaders of his day to know that pseudo-spirituality is a deadly disease — and a common and contagious one at that.

What Is a Right Understanding of Spiritual Life?

When someone asks you, "How is your spiritual life going?" what comes to mind? How do you define spirituality? How do you assess spiritual progress?

Amidst all the confusing and distorted notions, Scripture speaks with brilliant clarity. "Whoever claims to live in him must walk as Jesus did" (1 John 2:6). To pursue spiritual life means simply this: *To know Jesus more intimately and to live as if he were in your place.* It is to order your life in such a way that you stay connected to Christ, thinking as he thought, speaking as he spoke, and walking as he walked.

To pursue spiritual life means simply this: To know Jesus more intimately and to live as if he were in your place.

Certainly, this imitation of Christ will look different for each person, expressing itself through that person's unique temperament, abilities, and circumstances. But there is a common denominator. At the core of Jesus' teaching is the command to love God with all your heart, soul, mind, and strength, and to love other people as you love yourself (Mark 12:30–31).

When someone asks you how your spiritual life is going, the real question is, "Are you becoming more loving toward God and people?" Regardless of anything else you measure, how you stand up against that statement will reveal your true spiritual stature. This measurement is the supreme spiritual diagnostic for Christ-followers who want to please him.

Doing Life in Jesus' Name

What would this kind of life look like if you actually lived it out? Let's face it — you could chalk up this concept as another idea that sounds good but isn't really practical. Yet God is inviting you to make each moment of every day a chance to learn from him how to master the art of life.

The apostle Paul put it like this: "Whatever you do, whether in word or deed, do it all in the name of the Lord Jesus" (Col.3:17). In the Bible, names often reflect a person's character. So to do something in Jesus' name means to do it in a way consistent with his character—to do it the way Jesus himself would.   W W J D ?

Paul's teaching is very comprehensive on this matter. He says, "*Whatever* you do. . . ." And in case anyone misses his point, he adds, ". . . whether in *word* or *deed*. . . ." And in case anyone misses *that* he says, ". . . do it *all* in the name of the Lord Jesus" (italics added for emphasis).

Your spiritual life is simply your whole life—every minute and detail of it—from God's perspective. In other words, God isn't interested in your spiritual life. God is simply interested in your *life*. And every moment is an opportunity to do life in Jesus' name.

One fully devoted follower, Brother Lawrence, put it this way:

> . . . (W)hat makes you think that God is absent from the maintenance shop but present in the chapel? . . . Holiness doesn't depend on changing our jobs, *but in doing for God's sake what we have been used to doing for our own.*
>
> Seriously—repair the equipment for God, answer the abusive phone calls for God, concentrate fully on the job you're doing for God. He isn't obsessed with religion—he's the God of the whole of life. But we need to give it to him, consciously turning it over into his hands. Then whatever we're doing—provided it is not against his will—becomes an act of Christian service.
>
> —David Winter, *Closer Than a Brother*
> (on the life of Brother Lawrence)

God isn't interested in your spiritual life. God is simply interested in your life.

All of the everyday stuff of life can be filled with his presence—if you are. You *can* do what you're doing right now as Jesus would do it in your place. And if you do, you too will know the joy of true spiritual life.

SPIRITUAL EXERCISE

Here is an experiment for putting <u>Colossians 3:17</u> into practice. This week:

Memorize Paul's words in Colossians 3:17: "And <u>whatever you do</u>, whether in word or deed, <u>do it all in the name of the Lord Jesus,</u> giving thanks to God the Father through him."

Think about what it would mean for you to live the ordinary moments of your life as if Jesus were in your place. How would you do each of the following activities in Jesus' name?

- Waking up
- Greeting those you see first in the morning
- Eating
- Driving
- Working outside the home or caring for children while at home
- Shopping
- Watching TV
- Doing household tasks
- Reading the paper
- Going to sleep

Try it out. <u>Focus on Jesus' presence with you</u> as you go through the seemingly inconsequential moments of your day. Keep it simple; continually direct your thoughts back to him: ask for his help or his guidance, or simply share your heart with him.

Keep track of how the experiment goes. (If you don't already have a journal, we strongly recommend you start one so that you can keep a running list of observations throughout the duration of this study.) You will share your insights and experiences with the group when you meet.

BIBLE STUDY

1. Describe the picture Jesus paints in <u>John 10:10</u> of what should happen in the life of all who follow him. *The Shepherd and His Flock*

"The thief comes only to steal and kill and destroy; I have come that they may have life, and have it to the full."

The word picture of Jesus as the good shepherd shows us how He loves and cares for all the sheep, nurtures them daily, knows them individually by name, and is constantly watching out for their welfare. As they respond to His leading, they become partakers of His leadership; they have the freedom of going in and out + find pasture ... are saved and have life to the fullest.

— Jesus wants "the best" for us, His followers, for whom He lay down His life and rose again.

What has prevented you or other Christians you know from having that quality of life?

Life itself has become more complicated, and there are so many distractions available to take up our time and thoughts: TV, computers, cell phone games + chat lines; multiple sports activities (players + participants); beauty products, clothes, travel + entertainment.

2. Read <u>Matthew 23:1–28</u>. In this passage, Jesus has some harsh words for the religious leaders of his day. These scribes and Pharisees were well versed in Scripture and considered to be spiritually "in the know." If anyone understood what it meant to be spiritually mature, it was them—or so they (and those around them) thought. Yet Jesus was extremely frustrated by their <u>spiritual shallowness</u> and <u>obsession with externals.</u>

These "holy" men were teachers of the Law and were to be obeyed. Jesus said: "Do not do what they do, for they do not practice what they preach." They wished to be important in the eyes of men.

Jesus said: "The greatest among you will be your servant. For whoever exalts himself will be humbled, and whoever humbles himself will be exalted."

They gave a 10th, but neglected more important matters of the law: justice, mercy, + faithfulness. They are full of greed and self-indulgence. Beautiful on outside (appear as righteous), but inside are full of hypocrisy + wickedness.

What specific behaviors does Jesus confront?

v. 3 *they do not practice what they preach.*

v. 4 *they put heavy loads on men's shoulders, but are not willing to lift a finger to move them.*

v. 5 *they do things for show: love places of honor, important seats in synagogues* ⑥

NOTE: Phylacteries were little boxes with Scripture verses in them tied around the forehead—an obvious display of spiritual knowledge. The tassels on their garments were supposed to remind them to obey God (Num. 15:37–41), yet the Pharisees enlarged theirs to appear a bit superior.

vv. ⑥–7 *above*
love men to greet them + call them Rabbi

v. 13 *they shut the kingdom of heaven in men's faces*

v. 15 *travel far + wide to make a single convert, then make him twice as much a son of hell as you are.*

vv. 23–24 *neglected important matters of law: justice, mercy, and faithfulness.*
— strain out a gnat, but swallow a camel. *(take notice of minor things, but omit major problems)*

> NOTE: In those days, most everyone had little <u>herb gardens.</u> In an effort to be scrupulous, the teachers of the law and the Pharisees even <u>gave a tenth</u> of what those gardens produced. It would be like someone in our own day tithing on the dime they found on the street—not a bad thing, but petty in light of an <u>utter failure to focus on more important aspects</u> of justice, mercy, and faithfulness.

vv. 25–28 *they clean up what shows: outside of cup or dish but inside is full of greed + self-indulgence*
– like white washed tombs, look beautiful, inside full of men's bones + all unclean –
– outwardly appear righteous, but inside full of hypocrisy and wickedness

3. What heart attitude(s) do you think all these behaviors have in common?

– selfish, self-serving – "me" attitudes
– uncaring of general population's problems + no interest in truly bettering their lives
– need to be more open to letting God run our lives (not putting God in a box)
hind sight is 20/20 how you react when actually in situation!?

4. As you read through this passage, was there any point at which you said, "Ouch—I have a tendency in that direction"? How do you think such distorted views of spirituality have crept into your life?

23 – I remain silent when I should speak up about justice, mercy + faithfulness
– must refrain from being judgmental

5. In your opinion, why is it easy for people to think that acquiring knowledge, following formulas, and obeying rules will automatically lead to true spiritual maturity?

It's much easier to listen to God's word than to practice what it teaches.

6. According to the following words of Jesus, what must be at the heart of any concept of spirituality?

Matthew 23:11–12 *humility*
— greatest among you will be your servant.
— whoever exalts himself will be humbled —
our one teacher is Christ — perfect example

Mark 12:28–34 *(belief in triune God — Matt. 12:28 on)*
The most important commandments:
① v.30 — Love the Lord your God with all your heart ... soul, and ... mind, and with all your strength.
② v. 31 — Love your neighbor as yourself.
No commandment is greater than these.
— more important than all burnt offerings and sacrifice

John 15:4–17 (hint: look for repeated words or phrases)
v.4 No branch can bear fruit by itself; it must remain in the vine. Bear much fruit, showing yourselves as disciples.
God is the vine, we are the branches
v. 12 — Love each other as I have loved you.
13 — greater love has no one than this, that one lay down his life for his friends.
16 — You did not choose me, but chose you to go and bear fruit — fruit that will last.

7. Being as candid as possible, how would you assess the state of
   your spiritual life right now?

What work would you invite God to do?

Get better acquainted with my neighbors:
— now more of a nodding acquaintance
determine how I can be of help to them
and show caring in a positive way
— Help me to expand my church friendships
to better know + be able to pray for them

How can the members of your small group help?

Pray for me as I deal with various workmen
both here in Auburn + on Cape
— give me patience when I am discouraged
by their lack of response.

TAKE-AWAY

My summary of the main point of this session, and how it impacts . *has an impact*
me personally:

God should be our constant companion along each moment of every day, helping us to be aware of his direction and opportunities to help others.

Being available to others' needs rather than thinking of how we might benefit by certain actions.

Be genuine, not hypocritical

NOTE: You will fill in this information after your group discussion. Leave it blank until the conclusion of your meeting.

SESSION
TWO

GRACE

SESSION TWO

Grace

Reading by John Ortberg and Laurie Pederson

B ob is a great dad who wants his kids to learn about grace. Every once in a while, he lets his kids go free when they know they're about to be punished. When he does this, he'll say what they are receiving: "Grace. I'm cutting you some slack. I'm showing you grace. Do you know why I'm doing this?"

They shake their heads.

"No reason at all. There's never a reason for grace."

Once, his son Ryan had violated several important rules simultaneously and was about to receive justice. "Can't you cut me some grace?" he pleaded.

Bob, who was not in a gracious mood right at the moment, asked, "Why? Give me one good reason I should cut you some grace."

"Dad," his son said, somewhat shocked at his father's theological lapse, "there's *never* a reason for grace."

we don't earn it – its god's gift *Eph 2:8-9* *disagrees*

The Story of Two Sons—Luke 15:11–32

One of Jesus' unforgettable stories about grace is sometimes called the parable of the prodigal son. Henri Nouwen, in his book *The Return of the Prodigal Son*, points out it is really the story of *two* prodigal sons ... and one gracious father.

One son's lostness is obvious. A runaway who defiantly flees to a distant country looking for fulfillment he had not allowed himself to find at home, this son is the picture of obvious sinners—people who have deliberately pursued life and pleasure apart from God.

There's never a reason for grace.

Although less obvious, the older son is just as lost. On the surface this son did all the things good sons are supposed to do. He stayed home, worked hard, kept the rules, stayed within the lines. But he was, in his own way, far from home. Judgmental and jealous, his words reveal the inner complaint of a heart that felt it never received what it was due. He did not know joy, for joy and resentment cannot live in the same heart. This son is a picture of the religious leaders of the day—people whose very pursuit of righteousness left their hearts prideful, cold, and far from the Father. And they didn't even know they were lost.

One son wandered off. One stayed dutifully behind. Neither lived a life of abundance in the father's house.

One son wandered off. One stayed dutifully behind. Neither lived a life of abundance in the father's house.

The "Sons" in Each of Us

Is there a bit of the prodigal son in you? Are you tempted, even as a believer, to wander from home in search of self-fulfillment? Perhaps your wanderings are carefully disguised—maybe even religiously acceptable. But is there something that lures nonetheless? The desire for wealth or power? An appetite for achievement, admiration, status? A craving for physical gratification?

Nouwen understood these prodigal realities:

> *As long as we live within the world's delusions, our addictions condemn us to futile quests in "the distant country," leaving us to face an endless series of disillusionments while our sense of self remains unfulfilled. . . . I am the prodigal son every time I search for unconditional love where it cannot be found.*

It's an amazing truth: We are loved so much that we are free to leave home.

And what about the older son? The one who worked hard, kept the rules, and fulfilled his obligations only to become increasingly resentful and joyless. Might there be a bit of him in you? It's sad but true that many of us have an easier time being *saved* by grace than we do *liv-*

the older son

ing in grace. Over time, ours becomes a life of inner complaint. In our own way, we end up equally far from home.

Grace: An Invitation to Be "At Home" with the Father

The gracious Father desires only to bring his children home. He longs for each of us—older and younger sons alike—to walk back into his welcoming arms. He invites us to relax in his love, to feel his esteem, to be the recipient of a lifetime of lavish feasts at his table. He longs for us to live in grace.

The good news is that you really can grow to experience grace more and more. Grace starts with repentance and forgiveness and grows as we train our eyes to see the many aspects of the Father's everyday generosity often taken for granted—a warm home, a satisfying meal, the kind words of a good friend, the sight of a garden blooming in a riot of color, the body of Christ gathered in rich worship. Grace surrounds us every moment, but we must develop eyes to see.

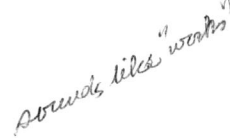
sounds like "works"

It's sad but true that many of us have an easier time being saved by grace than we do living in grace.

Finally, we grow in grace when we give ourselves permission to celebrate and enjoy life. For the grace-impaired among us, this actually takes some discipline and a new understanding. God has saturated the world with wholesome pleasures. Wholeheartedly enjoying them is not sinful. It's not frivolous. It is an irreplaceable part of spiritual life, an irreplaceable part of what it means to live in grace.

The father in the parable said it best: "Everything I have is yours." Linger on those words. Live with them. Your Father is saying them to *you*.

Extending Grace

For a long time I have lived with the insight that returning to my Father's home was the ultimate call. It has taken me much spiritual work to make the elder son as well as the younger son in me turn around and receive the welcoming love of the Father. The fact is that, on many levels, I am still returning. But the

*closer I come to home the clearer becomes the real-
ization that there is a call beyond the call to return....
I now see that the hands that forgive, console, heal,
and offer a festive meal must become my own.*

—Henri Nouwen, *The Return of the Prodigal Son*

God wants every day to be a homecoming. Only as we learn to live in the grace of the Father's house can we become like him. When our hands are filled with his blessings, we are able to relax our grip on our sinful pursuits of fulfillment, our prideful competitiveness, our inner complaints. Gradually, each of these is replaced with a refreshing freedom and vitality, and we become drawn to extend his grace-giving ways.

We extend God's grace each time we behave kindly and generously to others—when we pray for them, notice them, forgive them, serve them, include them. We extend God's grace especially through evangelism, which is simply sharing his life.

As we live in grace, we come to experience a joyful, unforced fruitfulness. In time, we find ourselves living more and more like Christ, who drank in the joy of his Father's house to the full and then offered it freely to others—for no reason at all, except grace.

*Only as we learn to live
in the grace of the
Father's house can we
become like him.*

SPIRITUAL EXERCISE

As before, experiment this week with living life as Jesus would if he were in your place; only this time, specifically focus on spending a day consciously "at home" with the Father—living in his grace. Here are some ideas:

- Wake up and direct your first thoughts to his loving presence.
- Pay attention to his gracious daily provisions, even the ordinary ones—a closet full of clothes, a hot shower, the ability to see, think, hear, and feel.
- Look for examples of his grace around you in scenes of natural beauty, the face of a friend, meaningful accomplishments, moments that make you laugh.
- When you sit down for a meal, imagine God preparing this table just for you. Slow down; enjoy the gift of food in his presence.
- Pursue a favorite activity. Try to consciously engage in it with your Father as your companion.
- When you fail, bring it honestly to him. Experience his open arms of forgiveness.

Does it make any difference to live this way? Is God's companionship enjoyable? Do you feel like your days are spent living freely in your Father's house? What did you find hindered your ability to enter into this kind of grace?

Read Luke 15:11–32 several times throughout the week. Use at least two translations if possible.

Reflect on this statement by Henri Nouwen that describes his own prodigal-son-like wanderings:

> *The farther I run away from the place where God dwells, the less I am able to hear the voice that calls me the Beloved, and the less I hear that voice, the more entangled I become in the manipulations and power games of the world.*

1. How have you seen this pattern played out in your life?

2. In what ways do you sometimes leave your Father's house as the younger son did?

Recently spent too much time being concerned with the things of this world, Cape exterminator and need for new roof — Auburn chimney, exhaust fan, yard work

What tends to pull you away from God?

3. Is there any way in which you may be like the dutiful but resentful older son?

I tend to think the Father might have told him (reminded him) how much his cooperation + good work was appreciated, not taken for granted. My daughter felt she was not encouraged enough along life's way, and thus she felt insecure + fearful that she wasn't doing enough to be worthy of our praise (and therefore, so God for giving her considerable talents)

4. How does being like the older son impact your desire to extend grace to others?

I want to have the eyes to see a need where my actions can make a difference. Many times even a kind word or smile can be what's needed at a particular time.

5. Read the following passages and put into your own words what God thinks of you and how he desires to lavish his kindness on you. Write your paraphrase as if God were personally speaking to you.

Ephesians 1:5–8

It was God's will that He loved us so much that before the world was formed, he chose us and made us blameless for all sin through Jesus' sacrifice of His life in our place. By His grace we are saved.

Ephesians 1:18–19

We have heard and believed the gospel of salvation and shown love to all saints. God gives us the spirit of wisdom, enlightens our heart to the hope for the future to be shared with God. His power is incredibly great.

Ephesians 2:12–13, 19

(heathen)

Romans 8:15–17

At one time the gentiles were called uncircumcized, separated from Christ, alienated from Israel, and strangers to gods promises. Now however you have been brought near by the blood of Christ. Now the 2 groups are fellow citizens + members in the household of God.

Those who live according to the Spirit set their minds doing things that please God. Setting their minds on the flesh is hostile to God. Rather than fear, we now have sonship. We call Abba, Father. And he responds that we are children of God, heirs, and suffer w/ him so

6. Reflect again on the father's words: "All that I have is yours."
   How would your life be different today if you really believed
   God meant those words for you? Be specific.

that we are also glorified w/ him.

Sometimes we are afraid to put our lives completely in gods hands. But he has promised to be with us all the time (good + bad) and He will be sure we will be burdened with more than we can bear (with his ever-available help)

Attitude of gratitude.

TAKE-AWAY

My summary of the main point of this session, and how it impacts me personally:

God wants us to be happy when a lost soul returns to the fold (as the younger son)

God's way is best, and we should be full of praise as He leads us each day and helps us depend on Him for all our needs.

We should be willing to help those around us — care about their knowing of God's sacrifice of His son for all believers who acknowledge their need for a savior — God's grace has been extended to us

Our future is promised to be with Him

NOTE: You will fill in this information after your group discussion. Leave it blank until the conclusion of your meeting.

The next session contains an extended solitude exercise in place of the usual Bible study and spiritual exercise. Be sure to give yourself plenty of time to complete that exercise before your group meeting.

SESSION
THREE

SESSION THREE

Growth

Reading by John Ortberg and Judson Poling

I magine your phone ringing one day. . . .
"This is the U.S. Olympic Committee. We have selected you to represent our country in the next Olympics. You will run the marathon. Billions of people will watch as you compete against the best runners in the world in a twenty-six-mile race for the gold."

There is a moment of stunned silence. *Your* idea of a "good run" is from the couch to the fridge during commercials. And the thought of wearing running shorts . . . well, it's not a pretty picture. But for some reason, once you catch your breath, you agree to do it.

If you were serious about competing, you'd have to enter into a life of training. You cannot run a marathon simply by going out and trying—not even by trying very hard. Instead, you must arrange your life around activities that will enable you to eventually do what you cannot (even with great willpower) do now.

This analogy is used by Paul in 1 Corinthians 9:24–27 and 1 Timothy 4:7–8, where he advises to "train yourself to be godly." The central idea of Paul's metaphor is that many people, when they hear about spiritual growth, think they must simply try harder to be like Jesus. So they try harder to be patient, or gentle, or kind, and it works no better than trying hard to run a marathon without training.

Instead, we are called to a life of spiritual training. This is not a burdensome thing—in fact, straining and overexertion do not help at all. To train spiritually means

> *You cannot run a marathon simply by going out and trying—not even by trying very hard.*

to engage in practices, experiences, and relationships that will help us to eventually do by training what we cannot do now just by trying hard.

Many people associate training with joyless, painful activities. They think training means to do something unpleasant in the hope that eventually you can really have fun. But while practicing piano scales or running football drills in the hot August sun may not be examples of enjoyable training, in the spiritual realm, training can be far less disagreeable. It can actually be pleasant—and the payoff enormously satisfying.

There are no limits to the number of training exercises in which we can engage; choosing them wisely will take discernment. With what particular temptations do I tend to struggle? What practices most help me live close to the Father? We know from Scripture—and it has been verified in the lives of millions of Christ-followers over the years—that some practices are especially foundational.

To train spiritually means to engage in practices and experiences that will help us to eventually do by training what we cannot do now just by trying hard.

Reading and Meditating on Scripture

This practice is not simply about acquiring Scripture knowledge. It is important, of course, to be familiar with the entire Bible, and sometimes you will need to read broadly. But in reading for transformation, you will need to go slowly. *Formation*—being conformed to Christ—must be your desire, not just information. Ultimately, the goal is not to get through the Scriptures, it's to get the Scriptures through *you*. And that will require meditation.

The act of meditation should not seem spooky; it simply involves the practice of sustained attention. Whatever your mind repeats, it retains. If you think about it, each of us daily gives sustained attention to something. It's just a question of what that something is.

Real growth comes when we take a basic truth of Scripture, such as "The Lord is my Shepherd," and meditate on it. What does it mean to have the Lord—the God of the universe—as *my* shepherd? How would this day, with all its anxieties, be different if I really believed that? What would it feel like to cease my frantic activity long enough to let my Shepherd restore my soul?

In time, as you reflect on Scripture, you will begin to hunger for a deeper knowledge of God as your Shepherd. As you do this, a signficant thing will happen. You will find that you really do want him to shepherd your life. He actually does a better job of it than you do. By taking in Scripture and then pondering it, lingering on it—chewing on it, so to speak—you will be feeding on the Word of God. You will be training your heart in a better way to live.

Solitude and Prayer

"In the morning, while it was still very dark, Jesus got up, left the house, and went off to a solitary place, where he prayed" (Mark 1:35). Mark tells us about Jesus' practice of solitude and prayer, something he returned to again and again during his earthly ministry. Solitude is a fundamental practice for those in pursuit of spiritual life.

Solitude allows you to leave behind the scaffolding of your life and find out what there is between you and God.

Solitude is often used to engage in other practices such as prayer, reflection, or self-examination. Often people go at it with an arsenal of books, tapes, CDs, and videos. But these are the very things you need to get away *from*. In its purest sense, solitude is not defined by what you do, but by what you *don't* do. It involves withdrawing from the people and noise and the chronic overstimulation of everyday life. Solitude liberates you from a constant state of hurriedness and harassment. It allows you to leave behind the scaffolding of your life and find out what there is between you and God.

In the quiet of solitude, we distance ourselves from the voices and influence of others to hear the "still, small voice of God." We cultivate an inward attentiveness and give God access to our lives. Through solitude we feed our souls.

Corporate Learning and Worship

Let him who cannot be alone beware of community....
Let him who is not in community beware of being
alone....

—Dietrich Bonhoeffer, *Life Together*

Just as we must pursue the stillness of solitude, we must seek the fellowship and accountability of community if we want to fully experience and express spiritual life. So we commit ourselves to coming together and submitting to the teaching of the Word. We also gather to worship God. We do this simply because God is worthy of our praise. In addition, God, in his grace, has decreed that in worship we are often encouraged and transformed in ways we could not be apart from this practice. In these corporate practices we root out self-absorption. We are reminded that we need and are a part of each other, that our life is about something bigger than just ourself.

The training process you embark on must be tailor-made for you and by you.

Your Personalized Growth Plan

The training process you embark on must be tailor-made for you and by you. There is no formula that works with everyone. Our creative God, who made all of us unique, will also uniquely *re*make us.

Consider this analogy: Every married couple needs to cultivate their relationship. One couple may like breakfast together once a week. Another couple has a date night. Another couple may have "check-in times" after the kids go down. Other couples do periodic weekends away with just the two of them. What every marriage has in common is the need for enrichment. But how that is played out is as unique as the couples themselves. "What works for *you*?" is the question to answer.

Great freedom and creativity is allowed — indeed, *needed* — for how you cultivate your relationship with Christ and your training to be more like him. So learn from what others are doing — but resist the temptation to compare yourself with them.

Marks of Growth

Many homes have a closet door with little measurements marked on the back of it. The door becomes a place where the growth of the children is tracked across time, inch by inch.

What is the unit for measuring spiritual growth? It is nothing less than Christlike character. As we become more loving, honorable, courageous, and integrity-filled people (like the fruit of the Spirit mentioned in Galatians 5:22), we know that spiritual growth is taking place, inch by inch.

The spiritual practices mentioned above (and others) must lead us to that kind of progress. And, above all, we must be mindful that without the fruit of love, any such practices are missing their mark.

SOLITUDE EXERCISE

Between now and when your group meets again, we invite you to engage in the training practices mentioned in this session. This week's exercise will require setting aside a time for solitude. Schedule a time (we suggest an hour minimally; a half-day would be better) when you will be fairly rested and alert. Find a place where you will be alone and free from distractions and interruptions. Make it a place where you can be comfortable and where, if possible, the setting is pleasing to you. Bring a journal or a pad of paper to record your thoughts and make any notes to yourself. Also, bring your Bible.

The steps below form a basic outline you can follow as you seek solitude. Adapt them according to the time you have. By all means, follow the Holy Spirit as he leads and prompts you. The goal is not just to complete an assignment; the goal is to quiet yourself before God, review his work in your life, and to hear the words he has just for you.

> NOTE: Read through this entire exercise before you begin. Be familiar with the movement and flow of the experience before you actually engage in it.

Still Yourself

One of the hardest things to do in our daily busyness is simply *stop*. Being quiet usually produces boredom, anxiety, or drowsiness. But in order to embark on this exercise, you must deliberately be still. That means your body is still, your mind stops racing, and your thoughts become directed instead of reactive.

People often struggle with distractions when they pray. A few minutes of preparation can help. Don't trouble yourself with what you have to do later or what happened yesterday. Connect with *right now*; put *soon* and *recently* out of your mind. You can think about all that later. If you need to, write down ideas that come to you, things to do, and "park them" on your pad of paper so they don't interfere with your concentration but you don't forget them, either.

Invite God's Presence

Now acknowledge that God is present with you. Thank him for his never-failing companionship. Place yourself in his hands. Ask him to help you be sensitive to his leadings. Invite him to speak to you in whatever way is most needed.

Focus Your Thoughts

Turn to Colossians 3:12–17 and read those verses several times. Don't try to dissect the passage. Don't worry about what you don't understand; concentrate on what's clear. Let the words speak to you in simplicity—let them "dwell in you richly."

Reflection and Personal Review

Keep your Bible open to Colossians 3. Use this passage as a verse-by-verse guide for a time of reflection and personal review. We've given you some thoughts to stimulate your thinking, but don't limit yourself to these. Speak freely to God, asking him to speak freely to you. Write down your observations as you go (unless writing becomes a hindrance to uninterrupted meditation).

"As God's chosen people, holy and dearly loved. . . ."

Imagine . . . the Sovereign God choosing you—knowing you, wanting you, pursuing you. Think back to the picture of the gracious father running to embrace the prodigal son. Picture God running to embrace you the very first time you repented—and every time since then. He has invited you to sit with him at a banquet in your honor. Imagine him declaring you forever perfect and holy in his eyes.

Ponder the thought that you are his beloved. Your presence and companionship matter to him. God wants to be with you at this very moment. He doesn't have to—but he desires you. What does that mean to you, even right now?

"Whatever you do, whether in word or deed, do it all in the name of the Lord Jesus. . . ."

Reflect on your spiritual journey recently—particularly as you have been consciously trying to live your everyday life "in Jesus' name." What work has God been doing in you?

It might be helpful to make a note of some of the specific times when you got it right—times when you:

- brought Jesus' love and grace to bear in a difficult situation;
- "clothed yourself" in compassion, kindness, or patience;
- exercised humility when it would have been easier to exercise self-promotion;
- extended forgiveness or brought Christ's spirit of peace and reconciliation to bear in a situation; or
- confronted a situation head-on when avoidance would have been easier.

Are you aware of any specific factors that helped you live like Jesus in those situations?

Take some time to reflect on the encouraging signs of growth. Consider every new step of faith, trust, or obedience. God's transforming work is happening inch-by-inch in your life. Can you imagine his delight? One of his beloved children (you!) is making progress. Here you are—this very minute—seeking him as best you know how. That's exactly what he died to make possible. Sit quietly and allow yourself to receive his words of affirmation.

Receive Forgiveness Anew

Continue using the passage from Colossians, but turn your attention to those areas needing correction. Reflect on the ways you have struggled, felt frustrated, or failed during the past month or so. Be specific and concrete. Were there direct acts of disobedience? Perhaps you neglected to do all that you could have lovingly done in a situation.

Do you notice any patterns in these experiences? Were there any common denominators: careless words, withholding love, spiritual timidity, a critical spirit, self-promotional tendencies, lust, greed, arrogance? What specific factors contributed to these less-than-successful attempts to live like Jesus?

Take a few moments to bring these areas to God in honest confession. Ask for his forgiveness, power, and help in each area.

Be sure you allow God to speak his words of forgiveness. If needed, refresh your mind with the truths of Psalm 103:8–14 and Philippians 1:6. Rest in God's grace and trust his unwavering commitment to you and your growth.

I am sure that he who began a good work in you will bring it to completion at the day of Jesus Christ. (the time of His return)

God's attributes: compassionate, gracious, slow to anger, full of loving kindness, will not keep His anger forever - He has not dealt with us according to our sins nor rewarded us according to our iniquities. His loving kindness is great toward these that revere Him, like a father of his children. As far as the east is from the west, he has forgiven us.

"Let the peace of Christ rule in your hearts. . . . be thankful. . . .sing psalms, hymns and spiritual songs with gratitude in your hearts to God. . . ."

Now allow grace to become gratitude. Let your thankfulness find full and free expression. Let God know—and hear yourself say—how grateful you are for all that fills your life. If you're able, even thank him that the difficulties you face can become places where he will meet you and show himself gracious on your behalf.

It can be helpful to bring your exercise to a definite close. A phrase like, "Thank you, Lord, for this time together; I now offer it up to you and invite you to walk with me throughout this day," can help create an ending point.

Review the Experience

Before you make the transition back into your daily activities, take a few minutes to reflect on what has just happened. What did you observe happening in yourself as you had this time of solitude? Did your mind wander? Did you talk to God about how hard it was to stay focused? Did it feel pleasant? What was the high point? When was it difficult? How would you summarize what happened if you had to tell someone about it right now?

TAKE-AWAY

My summary of the main point of this session, and how it impacts me personally:

I need to discipline myself
to begin the day with Bible reading
on a daily schedule
— at same time, same place,
in solitude w/o distraction
with time to meditate

Glenn + Heather
Eli — alone with brother gone
Toby is living with Heath — 3 weeks
& you cell phone bill (family)

her Grandmother — house broken in by
grandson (on drugs)
— bank calling him when
he comes in to cash check
900 - 1,000

David — good news — infection caused stomach pain
Sonja — bone spurs on knee
Jean's sister — not conversing on phone
just Email
daughter - 14 yr birthday party

NOTE: You will fill in this information after your group discussion. Leave it blank until the conclusion of your meeting.

Groups

Reading by John Ortberg

H ow very good and pleasant it is when brothers live together in unity" (Psalm 133:1).

The existence of community is the signature of God. God himself, as Trinity, experiences perfect oneness even as three Persons; and he made us in his image to be able to know oneness, too.

The existence of community is the signature of God.

Among other things, relationships have an amazing potential to transform our lives—for better or worse. One psychologist put it like this: "It takes people to make people sick, and it takes people to make people well."

Throughout the history of the church, all the way back to Jesus and his followers, any powerful work of the Spirit is always accompanied by a renewed experience of the transforming power of community. One of the ways we pursue this is by meeting together in small groups of people who are committed to each other's spiritual growth.

What Relationships Give

How do relationships help us become more like Christ? What must be true in order for our relational world to promote real spiritual growth? In his book *Changes That Heal*, Dr. Henry Cloud suggests that we consider two elements: grace and truth. They are traits that characterize Jesus Christ (John 1:14).

Grace expressed in the sphere of relationships involves radical acceptance. It means we are embraced even with our shortcomings and failures. Grace allows us to come out of hiding and bring our weaknesses into the healing light of another's gaze. Grace reflects Christ's forgiving nature.

Truth equally reflects Christ's nature, but emphasizes the aspects of holiness and righteousness. Truth presents us with a sense of Christ's direction and boundaries to keep us from falling further into sinful and destructive patterns. Truth in our relational world confronts the unfortunate tendencies we all manifest toward self-deception.

Of course, from a biblical perspective, these aspects of Christ's nature are inseparable—both grace and truth are simultaneously and eternally present in him. And if we want to live as if Christ were in our place, we must become people of both grace and truth. But it is a challenging blend to sustain!

The Gracious Truth-Avoider

If we want to live as if Christ were in our place, we must become people of both grace and truth.

For some people, words of encouragement and affirmation flow easily, but there is fear of truth-telling if it involves confrontation. They prefer the comfort of avoidance. They tend to pretend a lot—that things are okay, that someone's sin doesn't matter, that they are not really angry. They may be thought of (and think of themselves) as loving persons, but they are missing truth—an essential element of community and spiritual transformation.

The "Grace-Less" Truth-Inflicter

On the other side of the continuum are those more ready to confront. To their credit, they don't want to pretend, and they take growth very seriously. However, too little effort is often put into speaking the truth in love (Eph. 4:15). They can tend to lack empathy—the ability and willingness to put themselves in another's place. In standing up for what's right, their very love of the truth may overshadow a spirit of love for the recipient of that truth.

A Community of Grace and Truth

The Fall took who we really were and who we really were created to be and separated that person from

God and others. That real person today longs for relationship and healing, but is unable to come into either one unless grace and truth are experienced together.

—Dr. Henry Cloud, *Changes That Heal*

Relationships that genuinely transform are characterized by grace and truth flowing freely over time. Only in the shelter of grace are we free to bring our weaknesses out of hiding and move beyond the pretense that exists even—or sometimes, especially—in the church. Only in the light of truth can we move beyond self-deception and find direction to live life differently, as God designed it.

God has an infinite number of ways to break through into our lives with his message of truth and grace. (He knew just the right combination needed to bring you to himself!) Yet it is sobering to realize how often he chooses to work through a community of flawed and finite people—a community that now includes you. It's risky business. He is trusting us to exercise wisdom and discernment. He is relying on us to walk with him and be attentive to his leadings and promptings throughout our day.

Relationships that genuinely transform are characterized by grace and truth flowing freely over time.

When grace and truth flow freely, people realize the full potential of human life as God designed it and as Jesus lived it. In those kind of relationships, progressive depth and self-disclosure become possible. And that's crucial for spiritual transformation. Even the simple act of offering counsel to one another becomes more valuable, because guidance rooted in truth is far more likely to hit the mark; when offered with grace, it's more likely to be heeded.

Is it any wonder that this kind of relating has the ability to transform not only individuals but also entire communities? It may start with only two people and spread throughout a small group. Eventually, whole churches can become fertile seedbeds of God-honoring life without pretense.

This is why group life—and all relationships—need to be characterized by grace and truth. And it is why your life must manifest these qualities as well.

SPIRITUAL EXERCISE

Continue with the experiment to live your normal week in Jesus' name. As you attempt to live as Jesus would live, be especially attentive to God's promptings to be an agent of truth and grace throughout your day. In relating with family, friends, coworkers, and even to those outside your normal sphere of relationships, do you sense any nudges from the Holy Spirit to:

- Write a note of affirmation or encouragement to someone?
- Tangibly reassure someone who is struggling spiritually?
- Lovingly raise a concern?
- Confront a situation with both honesty and grace?
- Initiate a conversation about God with a seeker?

Keep notes of your observations. How did those around you respond to your attempts at being gracious? What about when you tried to be truthful? Which came easier for you? Were there any times when you were the recipient of grace or truth? What was your response? Do you sense there is any message of truth or grace that God is trying to get across to you this week?

BIBLE STUDY

1. Jesus knew how to comfort the disturbed—and, when necessary, how to disturb the comfortable. Review the following passages and make a note of the ways he brought truth, grace, or both to the individuals he encountered.

John 8:3–11 *woman caught in adultery – stone her? Jesus wrote on ground — Whoever is without sin, stone her "said" Where are they who condemn you? Neither do I – Truth to all — with accountability to her. Sin no more –*

Luke 18:18–27 *Rich ruler – what must I do to inherit eternal life. Jesus – you still lack one thing – give away treasures + follow me. Camel + eye of needle – money is not security! good – didn't do it – Opportunity for grace – Told the truth --- faith in unseen was not possible for him*

Mark 7:5–8 *Disciples didn't obey rules. Audience – pharisees told them truth about legalism [today need for change to accomodate people's needs + computers, etc. electric guitar*

Luke 7:36–50 *sinful woman Pharisee's house – woman with perfume – she loved much — your faith has saved you 4 audiences – woman Simon - apostle house others in house how they relate to Him how they relate to each other Simon – in the middle truth + grace*

Luke 23:32, 39–43 *2 criminals also to be executed I man said – Jesus remember me when you go to your criminal speaks the truth — we are guilty, but you have done no wrong. Jesus said – Today you will be with me*

2. What pattern do you observe through Jesus' various interactions in the passages above? What was true about all those who received his words of grace? In what circumstances and with what kind of audience did Jesus most often dispense confrontive, unvarnished truth? (See also Luke 18:9–14.) *most confrontational? the self righteous – pharisees (often tried to make (in small settings more often) (hypocrites) him look bad in front of others. lots of questions!*

3. Now assess your own relating patterns. Toward which side of the Grace–Truth continuum do you lean? How is this tendency manifested in:

• Your job

• Your marriage/family life

• Your friendships

• Your small group

• Your relationship with God

• The way you treat yourself

Consider asking some of these individuals for *their* perception.

4. If you lean toward the truth-telling side, what valuable reminders do the following verses have for you?

Ephesians 4:32 *forgiveness, kindness, positive-ness be constructive when presenting truth*

Luke 6:41–42

1 Thessalonians 5:11, 14

5. If you lean toward the grace-giving side, how do these verses speak to your situation?

Luke 17:3

2 Timothy 1:7

2 Timothy 4:2

6. It has been said that one of the most difficult things to do is to be right without being hurtful. With this in mind, read Ephesians 4:15, 25, 29–32. What are some very concrete ways to express truth—even difficult truth—in gracious ways? How is it possible to confront and still build up? (Perhaps it would help to think of what you wish would be true when someone confronts you.)

7. Who in your life is a person who exudes grace? Who do you count on for truth? Does anyone around you display both in a healthy balance? *Dave Backlin — you're right I didn't think of it* *Bob Clave big, bad Bob* *Sonja Pastor Kohl Louis Backlin — sent cards to all political people of world* *Heath — Jeanne picked*

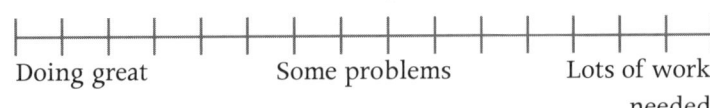

8. Finally, how about our group: How are we doing at being gracious with each other? How are we doing at truth-telling with each other?

Grace-giving

Doing great   Some problems   Lots of work needed

Comments:

Truth-telling

| | | | | | | | | | | | | | | | | |
Doing great   Some problems   Lots of work
needed

Comments:

TAKE-AWAY

My summary of the main point of this session, and how it impacts me personally:

> NOTE: You will fill in this information after your group discussion. Leave it blank until the conclusion of your meeting.

SESSION
FIVE

Gifts

Reading by John Ortberg

M any years ago, my grandfather phoned my mother and offered her some dishes. My grandmother had recently died, and he found a box full of old blue dishes in the attic. He was going to give them to the Salvation Army until he remembered that my mother liked the color blue, so he thought he'd see if she had a use for them.

The gift never made it out of the box.

She went into the attic expecting junk and found instead beautiful, handcrafted china with a forget-me-not pattern, twenty-four-carat gold trim, and inlaid mother-of-pearl cups. They had been made in a factory in Bavaria that was destroyed in World War II, so they were literally irreplaceable. And she had never seen them before.

Over the next few months, she and my father pieced together the story: My grandmother had received a dish here or a cup there growing up. They were so valuable that she put them in a box and waited for an occasion special enough to warrant using them. But in true Swedish fashion, nothing that special ever happened. The gift never made it out of the box.

Community Built on Gifts

The Bible says that God is the ultimate gift-giver; in fact, it calls him the giver of "every good and perfect gift" (James 1:17). It also says that God has given to all who follow him spiritual gifts, which enable them to serve others in the body of Christ.

The apostle Paul describes spiritual gifts in 1 Corinthians 12. He says there are a variety of gifts, but the same Holy Spirit; a variety of ministries (ways gifts can be expressed), but the same Lord; a variety of effects or results, but the same God.

Paul's words in verse 7 are critically important: "... to each one the manifestation of the Sprit is given for the common good." *To each one.* In the community of the people of God, everyone is gifted, whether those gifts are obvious and public, or private and behind-the-scenes. Simply put, God has made you a specialist in some area of ministry, and he is calling you to be a minister with your gifts.

Many churches today are still functioning under the model where members view the pastor, and perhaps a few staff members, as the ministers. The common assumption is that these people have a special relationship with God that others don't have, therefore it's up to them to do the work of the church. This thinking has left the modern church weak and crippled with overworked pastors or staff and a boatload of unmet needs.

Have you taken your gifts out of storage?

Do you see yourself as a minister? Have you taken your gifts out of storage? Are you polishing them and putting them to use? The word *gift* often carries the idea of something that's optional—a frill. But spiritual gifts are not luxuries. They are an absolute necessity for the life and health of the church.

Community Built on Servanthood

Not only must our gifts be used, but they must be used as Christ would use them—with a servant's spirit. Our spiritual gifts comprise a great treasure deposited within us—yet it is treasure "in jars of clay" (2 Cor. 4:7). Like the fine dishes in the story above, our gifts must get out of the container. But our containers are flawed. Competitiveness, envy, self-promotion, and the craving for approval mar us, even (and sometimes especially) when we step up to serve in the body of Christ.

Only if we adopt Christ's self-sacrificing lifestyle can we use our gifts the way they were designed to be used.

Biblical community occurs only when we imitate the Giver while exercising the gift. But how, with all our sinful and self-centered tendencies, do we get to that place of servanthood?

It is one of Scripture's great paradoxes that the very use of our gifts in servanthood helps progressively shape the heart of a servant in us. We are not called to serve just because of what it will do for the church; we are called to serve because of what it will do for *us*. Servanthood is a powerful practice for personal transformation.

Choosing to Serve vs. Being a Servant

Take a look at the scene that unfolds in John 13:1–17. When the disciples gathered for the Last Supper, Jesus wanted to teach them about servanthood. As they awaited dinner, they knew (as anyone of that day would) that someone needed to start washing feet. This was a role that clearly belonged to "the least." Most of us can adjust to the fact that we are not the greatest, but we certainly don't want to be the least. So the disciples sat with mud-caked feet ... until Jesus picked up a towel and a wash bowl. With that single act of humility, he forever redefined greatness.

Humility. It is one of God's most treasured virtues. And when it comes to the growth of humility, serving is one of the most important training exercises in which we can engage. Consider the words of Richard Foster, from his book *Celebration of Discipline*:

> *Of all the classical Spiritual Disciplines, service is the most conducive to the growth of humility. . . . Nothing disciplines the inordinate desires of the flesh like service, and nothing transforms the desires of the flesh like serving in hiddenness. The flesh whines against service but screams against hidden service. It strains and pulls for honor and recognition. . . . If we stoutly refuse to give in to this lust of the flesh we crucify it. Every time we crucify the flesh we crucify our pride and arrogance.*

Biblical community occurs only when we imitate the Giver while exercising the gift.

Foster goes on to draw an important distinction between *choosing to serve* and *being a servant*. When we choose to serve, we view service as an occasional option. We stay firmly in control. We decide whom, when, and under what conditions we will serve. Sometimes we are drawn to big acts to increase our sense of significance, and sometimes to lowly acts to guarantee a humble image. In any case, if our efforts are not adequately rewarded, we soon withdraw them altogether. Ironically, this so-called servanthood often fractures the very community it's intended to serve.

Conversely, *being a servant* involves the opening of ourselves to the promptings of the Holy Spirit. We relax our grip on our need to stay in firm control. Big acts of service and small are embraced with equal joy. And while affirmation received from others may be genuinely appreciated, we are content serving an audience of One.

Of course, as Christ modeled, there are always times when it is appropriate not to serve, times to let others serve us. Periodically being on the receiving end can, in itself, teach humility to a self-reliant heart. Increasingly, however, the trajectory of our life needs to move toward the mind-set and practice of serving others. Jesus calls each of us to this ministry of the towel. It has as much to do with the work he is trying to do *in us* as the work he is trying to do *through* us.

Jesus calls each of us to this ministry of the towel. It has as much to do with the work he is trying to do in us as the work he is trying to do through us.

SPIRITUAL EXERCISE

Continue with the experiment of living every day in Jesus' name. This week, deliberately focus on what it means to be a servant. Try to let go of your tendency to stay firmly in control of your service. Open yourself to letting him freely use you! This is not limited to certain spiritual activities or involvements. Every moment is an opportunity to reflect Christ's servanthood. Here are just a few ideas:

- Begin each morning by inviting God to use you through this day. Express your desire to be a servant in his name. Walk through the main events of your day with God in prayer.
- Make yourself available to be used at home. Look for some way you could be of service to those with whom you live.
- Throughout the day, as you begin a conversation, ask God to show you how you can best serve in that moment. Listen for his promptings to encourage, speak truth, and listen.
- Pour yourself out at work this week. Do your work with diligence, as if you were working directly for Christ. Serve a coworker.
- Ask God to specifically energize your gifts and abilities to serve his church this week.
- Stretch yourself to serve someone who you find difficult to serve.
- Engage in some acts of secret service. Write an anonymous note of encouragement; make an anonymous gift; do a task for someone but don't tell him or her you're the one who did it.

Keep track of how the week goes. What difference did it make to live your week this way? When was servanthood especially joyful? When was it most difficult? How easy was it for you to let go of your need to control your acts of service? How did the desire for recognition rear its head?

1. Reflect on the following statement: "I don't care if I'm not the greatest—just so I'm not the least." When is this true of you? How can this attitude affect your service to others?

   Good works are prompted by God ... and we should act upon them whenever opportunity occurs

2. Read Matthew 6:1–4 and contrast it with Matthew 5:14–16. What is the difference between self-promotion and an appropriate desire for having your deeds be seen?

   Do not do good things in order to be noticed. Rather, when you do things to benefit others, do it in secret and God will reward you.
   Jesus said we are the light of the world - As it shines before men, they will see your good works & glorify the father who is in heaven.

3. When are you most likely to manifest a strong need to be noticed as you serve? Is recognition always wrong? Why or why not?

   When you are feeling alone & foresaken - of no good to anyone

James + John — sons of Zebedee

4. In Matthew 20:25–28, Jesus commends service—and uses himself as an example to copy. What do people often do that Jesus prohibits in this passage? Give an example from your own experience of a time you fell into that trap.

Mother asked that 2 sons — one may sit on left and one on your right --- Whoever wishes to be great shall be your servant.

√ playing tennis in college

5. What is the connection between servanthood and being humble? (Matt. 23:11–12)   *pg. 1543*

10 – do not be called leaders, for One is your Leader— Christ!
11 – the greatest among you shall be your servant.
12 – whoever exalts himself shall be humbled and whoever humbles himself shall be exalted —

6. Describe a time when you "chose to serve" (as described in the reading). What attitudes and behavior characterized that experience?

Thanksgiving at church. The togetherness and fellowship experienced was its own "reward" — both to givers + recipients who shared experience.

What were the results? (Consider those you served as well as the impact on you personally.)

Now describe a time when you gave yourself freely as a servant. What attitudes and behaviors were true in that case?

babysitter — inconvenient, yet filled a great need so glad to be of service w/o complaint.

What were the results?

What concrete factors most help you to be a Spirit-led servant instead of a pseudo-servant?

picture yourself being the one in need ... helps you to fulfill the need willingly and happily.
Be willing to offer help when it seems appropriate BEFORE being asked

pg- 1836

7. Read Philippians 2:1–11. Answer the following questions based on that passage:

What does the "like-mindedness" and "oneness" Paul talks about contribute to our ability to serve one another (v. 2)?

The fellowship of the spirit, intent on one purpose with affection and love makes Paul's joy complete. Humility expressed as we consider others more important than ourselves. Christ humbled Himself by becoming obedient to the point of death on the cross for us.

Is it really true that others are better than you (v. 3)?

If god said so, it is truth.

What is Paul's point? *Christ is to be exalted — at the name of Jesus, every knee should bow, and every tongue confess the Jesus is Lord.*

How can seeing the two very different ways Christ lived (his exalted existence in heaven and then his humble dwelling among us on earth) help us be better servants (vv. 6–7)? (See also 2 Cor. 8:9.) *pg. 1812 Jesus Christ was rich (in heaven) but became poor so through His poverty we become rich*

What would be an analogy in your own life to these two positions or ranks?

Compare Christ's exaltation (vv. 9–11) with our promise of future rewards (such as hearing "Well done, good and faithful servant," as in Matthew 25:21). How can that motivate us to serve one another?

TAKE-AWAY

My summary of the main point of this session, and how it impacts me personally:

NOTE: You will fill in this information after you discuss this lesson in your group. Leave it blank until the conclusion of your meeting.

SESSION SIX

GIVING

Giving

Reading adapted from a message by John Ortberg

We are all treasuring creatures. The question is not *if* we treasure, only *what*. In his book *It Was On Fire When I Lay Down on It*, author Robert Fulghum describes a time when he learned a lesson about treasures.

His daughter Molly, just of school age, had become enthusiastic about packing the day's lunches for her brothers and father. One morning she handed her father two bags as he was about to leave—one regular lunch sack and one secured with duct tape, staples, and paper clips. In a hurry to get to work, he did not press for an explanation.

That afternoon, while hurriedly eating his lunch, he tore open the well-secured bag Molly had given him and shook out the contents. Out spilled two hair ribbons, three small stones, a plastic dinosaur, a pencil stub, a tiny seashell, and a handful of other childish articles.

Momentarily charmed, he hustled off to the important business of the afternoon, sweeping both brown bags into the wastebasket—leftover lunch, Molly's junk, and all. "There wasn't anything there I needed," he thought. Fulghum recalls the discussion that ensued at home that night:

"Where's my bag?"

"What bag?"

"You know, the one I gave you this morning."

> We are all treasuring creatures. The question is not if *we treasure, only* what.

"I left it at the office, why?"

"Those are my things in the sack, Daddy, the ones I really like — I thought you might like to play with them, but now I want them back."

"Oh."

And also — "uh-oh."

Molly had given me her treasures. All that a seven-year-old held dear. Love in a paper sack. And I had missed it. Not only missed it, but had thrown it in the wastebasket because "there wasn't anything in there I needed." . . . It wasn't the first or the last time I felt my Daddy Permit was about to run out.

That night, Fulghum made a long trek back to the office, arriving just ahead of the janitor. Combing through the trash can, one by one he retrieved the crumpled bag and its treasures, now dotted with mustard and smelling of onions. He carried them home carefully and returned them to Molly the next day. No questions were asked or explanations given.

He thought that was the end of the bag thing, but it wasn't.

To my surprise, Molly gave the bag to me once again several days later. Same ratty bag. Same stuff inside. I felt forgiven. And trusted. And loved. . . . Over several months the bag went with me from time to time. It was never clear to me why I did or did not get it on a given day. I began to think of it as the Daddy Prize and tried to be good the night before so I might be given it the next morning.

In time Molly turned her attention to other things . . . found other treasures . . . lost interest in the game . . . grew up. . . . Me? I was left holding the bag. She gave it to me one morning and never asked for its return.

So the worn paper sack is there in [my] box. Left over from a time when a child said, "Here — this is the best I've got. Take it — it's yours. Such as I have, give I to thee."

"Here — this is the best I've got. Take it — it's yours. Such as I have, give I to thee."

PURSUING SPIRITUAL TRANSFORMATION

Your Treasure and Your Heart

Our treasures are those things to which we assign great value. We think about them a lot. We hold them dear. We guard them. We prize them. We arrange our lives around trying to obtain and retain what we treasure.

I have my own little bag of treasures, and so do you. You decide what will go into it. Maybe it's a house or a car or jewels or clothes. Maybe your treasures are expensive, or maybe they wouldn't be worth anything to anybody but you.

Jesus warned, be careful what you put in your bag:

> *Do not store up for yourselves treasure on earth, where moth and rust destroy, and where thieves break in and steal. But store up for yourselves treasures in heaven, where moth and rust do not destroy, and where thieves do not break in and steal. For where your treasure is, there your heart will be also.*
>
> —Matthew 6:19–21

When you get close to someone's treasure, you've gotten very close to the core of their soul.

Whatever you treasure — whatever is in the bag — that is where your heart will be. Jesus doesn't say this to make us feel bad. He's just stating the way things are. When you get close to someone's treasure, you've gotten very close to the core of their soul.

What Does God Treasure?

The goal of every heart ought to be to treasure that which is treasured by God. So what does God treasure?

In Genesis, it says repeatedly that as God was creating, he would pause and reflect and declare, "It is good." But when he got to making the man and the woman, he exclaimed, "It is very good." The good of creation became *very* good when human beings were placed in it.

Supremely among everything else, God prizes people — the only creatures who possess his image. He treasures our individuality and our diversity — every language, every ethnic group, every culture. His love is so expansive, he died for us all.

Being a follower of Jesus requires cultivating the kind of heart Jesus had for people—especially the poor, the hungry, those without power, those who are victims of injustice. It means extending our love and support regardless of race or culture. It involves building up and extending his church through helping lost people hear about and embrace the good news of the gospel of Christ.

We must be Christ's hands and feet in treasuring all human beings.

Revealing and Shaping Your Heart

How does God's treasuring of people compare with what you treasure these days? How close are you to fully embracing God's priorities?

We must be Christ's hands and feet in treasuring all human beings.

To answer this question quite objectively, at least when it comes to your material resources, open your checkbook. Pull out your credit card statements. Review where your money is going these days. Then ask: "Does the way I invest my treasures reflect the values Jesus taught and lived? Is my generosity modeling his? Has it grown or declined in the past year?"

Jesus said more about money and possessions than almost any other topic. He understood that a person's attitudes and habits concerning money are the concrete expression of what a person treasures. They reveal your heart.

But there is something else that is true about treasures: not only do they reveal your heart, they shape it as well.

Our hearts are naturally shaped by greed and possessiveness. We are by nature clutchers. "Mine" is one of the first words a child learns. If we want to have hearts reshaped in the image of Christ, we need to train them, to regularly engage in exercises that will help us do what we cannot do by willpower alone. We need a tangible practice that will help us say, "Money, you cannot be the god of my life today."

Giving is just such a practice. One of the main reasons Scripture places so much emphasis on giving is that regularly opening your hands and parting with material resources is one of God's most important training exercises for reshaping your heart.

Every time you write a check to advance God's work, you remind yourself that he is on the throne, not money. Every time you give money or possessions to assist the poor or afflicted, you train your heart to trust God—even when trust doesn't come easy or feel natural. Every time you engage in an act of spontaneous generosity, you declare that God is your treasure, not your possessions.

A Standard of Living or a Standard of Giving?

Life in the world is preoccupied with increasing your standard of living. Life in the kingdom of God is preoccupied with increasing your standard of *giving*. This is not because God wants your money. It is not because he wants your possessions. It is because he wants your heart. He wants your love. He wants your trust. Those are his greatest treasures.

Life in the world is preoccupied with increasing your standard of living. Life in the kingdom of God is preoccupied with increasing your standard of giving.

In the end, the question of good stewardship is simply this: Will you come to him with your little bag—whatever is in it—and with childlike love say, "Here it is. This is the best I've got. Take it—it's yours. Such as I have, give I to thee"?

When Jesus hung on the cross, that is exactly what he said to you.

SPIRITUAL EXERCISE

Take a moment to pull a bill from your wallet. Notice the words "In God We Trust." (Imagine them written on your credit cards and checks too!) This week, every time you pull out a bill (or your credit card or a check), pause for a moment to:

- Thank God for the simple fact that he has entrusted you with those financial resources.
- Ask yourself, "Is the way I'm about to spend this money leading me toward greater trust in God? Is it moving my heart closer to treasuring what God treasures, or am I setting myself up to treasure other things?"
- When you do spend money on yourself, even if it's not a necessity, thank God and use that gift in his name as a reminder of his grace.
- Reflect on the fact God is trusting you. He is counting on you to further his purposes with the resources he has given you. He won't force your hand, but he earnestly desires it to open up and share readily.

As you go throughout your activities this week, listen to conversations—your own and those around you. What attitudes toward material possessions do they reveal? How many times are possessions equated with fulfillment? How much energy is focused around cars, clothes, houses, or other possessions? Keep a log of your observations.

BIBLE STUDY

1. In Matthew 13:44–46, Jesus tells two parables—one of a hidden treasure and one of a costly pearl. Carefully review both parables. What common threads hold the two together?

> *Kingdom of heaven is like a treasure hidden in the field which a man found and hid again. And from joy over it he goes and sells all that he has and buys that field.*
>
> *Again, the kingdom of heaven is like a merchant seeking fine pearls. And upon finding one pearl of great value, he went and sold all that he had and bought it.*

Did these men make sacrifices or investments? Explain your answer.

NOTE: These parables are often misunderstood as examples of self-surrender and sacrifice. But that misses the point. These stories are not a harsh call to heroic action; they are a simple statement about relative value. The kingdom of God is the "buy" of a lifetime. Stumbling on it, any sane investor would gladly cash out of lesser holdings to buy it. In the words of author Randy Alcorn, "This is like a child given the chance to trade bubble gum for a new bicycle, or a man offered ownership of the Coca-Cola company in exchange for a sack of bottle caps." Author John White says this of the lucky merchant: "There is nothing noble about his sacrifice. There would on the other hand be something incredibly stupid about not making it. . . . Everyone will envy him for his good fortune and commend him not on his spiritual character but on his common sense."

Do you think pursuing the kingdom really is worth it?

How would your lifestyle — and especially the use of your material resources — be different if you really believed that?

2. Scripture does not ask us to literally abandon all our possessions to follow Christ. According to the following verses, what *is* asked of us?

Deuteronomy 8:6–18

Keep commandments of the Lord your God to walk in His ways and to fear Him.
You shall bless the Lord your God for the good land which He has given you.
You shall remember the Lord your God

1 Timothy 6:6–10

8- If we have food and covering, with these we shall be content.
9- But those that want to get rich fall into temptation
... which plunge men into ruin and destruction.
10- Love of money is root of all sorts of evil ... Some have wandered from the faith and pierced themselves with many griefs; for it is He who is giving you power to make wealth; that May confirm His covenant which He swore to you fathers

1 Timothy 6:17–19. *Instruct those who are rich in this present world not to be conceited or fix their hope on the uncertainty of riches but on God, who richly supplies us with all things to enjoy. He Himself has said "I will never desert you, nor will I ever forsake you –*

Hebrews 13:5 *Make sure that your character is free from the love of money, being content with what you have*

3. Second Corinthians 9:6–15 is a classic text on Christian giving. Review the passage and then summarize each principle and promise associated with giving. *god gives most*

Principles (why to give, how to give, etc.)
He who sows sparingly will also reap sparingly. He who sows bountifully will also reap bountifully. god loves a cheerful giver
— fully supplying the needs of the saints. also overflowing through many thanksgivings to god

Promises (the results of giving)
god is able to make all grace abound to you, so that all grace abound to you so that always having all sufficiently in everything, you may have an abundance for every good deed
— they will glorify god for your obedience to your belief of the gospel of christ
— they will pray on your behalf

In what ways, if any, have you experienced the truths of this passage?

4. The reading suggests that what we do with our material treasures both *reveals* our heart and *shapes* our heart. Taking an honest look over the past year, what do your material treasures reveal about the preoccupations of your heart?

In what ways have your treasures shaped your heart—either positively or negatively?

5. How can Jesus' words in <u>Matthew 25:34</u>−40 help you assess what you truly value in your life these days?

When Jesus comes in His glory, all nations well be gathered before Him & He will separate them ... and say "Come, you who are blest of my Father inherit the kingdom prepared for you I was hungry — thirsty ... a stranger ... naked ... sick ... in prison what you did for one of these brothers of mine, you did it for me.

6. What do you think it means to "seek first [God's] kingdom and his righteousness" (Matt. 6:33) with respect to money and possessions? *✓ and all these things will be added to you*

Put into your own words the promise of the last part of that verse.

On a scale of 1 to 10, how close are you to really believing that promise?

7. Consider once again the words Robert Fulghum used to describe his daughter Molly's entrustment of her treasures to him: "Here — this is the best I've got. Take it — it's yours. Such as I have, give I to thee."

Reflect for a moment on Jesus' saying those words to you as he hung on the cross. What thoughts and feelings does that stir?

What would it take for you to genuinely say those words back to Jesus with respect to all that you treasure?

TAKE-AWAY

My summary of the main point of this session, and how it impacts me personally:

All we have is from God —
Anything we give away was also from God originally.

Toby — difficult time
Sonja
Ed + job
Cheryl + kids and sports takeover

> NOTE: You will fill in this information after you discuss this lesson in your group. Leave it blank until the conclusion of your meeting.

SESSION SEVEN

"We Know Him Well . . ."

Reading adapted from Laurie Pederson
and Judson Poling

We have come full circle to the original question of this study: "What does it mean to be truly spiritual?" What does it mean to "seek first" life in the kingdom of God (Matt. 6:33)? *and all these things will be added to you* *cue for: anxiety*

The answer? Simply put, it is to live in rich community with the Father—to drink in his love, his gifts, his power. Then, in grateful response, we are to seek what he seeks, prize what he prizes, live as he would live if he were in our place. Spirituality is not a compartmentalized pursuit, but one that enfolds every relationship, every emotion, every daily experience, from the most significant to the most mundane.

> *Spirituality is not a compartmentalized pursuit, but one that enfolds every relationship, every emotion, every daily experience, from the most significant to the most mundane.*

A Story to Remember

In his book *Windows of the Soul,* author Ken Gire tells of one man who lived this ideal. Though removed from us by time and distance, this man's life is a picture of what should happen to those who are seized by this simple but compelling view of what it means to follow the Master.

> *He was an English missionary in India whose mission board required him to keep detailed financial records for which he had to be skilled at double-entry bookkeeping. Which he wasn't. He had no background in accounting or business. He only had a calling. To be a missionary. But his balances were always off, and the separate accounts he was supposed to keep kept*

getting mixed, and so the mission board released him. Unfit for the mission field, was their assessment, when in truth, he was only unfit for bookkeeping. He left without incident. Nobody knew where.

Years later, a woman missionary visited a remote jungle village to introduce the natives to Jesus. She told them of His kindness and His love for the poor, how He went to their home to eat with them, how He visited them when they were sick, how He fed the hungry, healed the sick, bound up the wounds of the brokenhearted, and how children loved to follow Him.

The eyes of the natives lit up, their faces beamed, and one of them exclaimed: "Miss Sahib, we know him well; he has been living here for years!"

When they took her to see him, it was the man who years earlier had been dismissed by the mission board. He had settled there to do his work, sequestered from the double-entried tyranny of bookkeeping. Whenever anyone was sick, he visited them and waited up all night outside their hut if necessary, checking on them, tending to their needs. When they were hurt, he nursed their wounds. For the old and the infirm, he brought food and water. When cholera broke out in the village, he went from hut to hut, doing what he could to help.

I wonder. If someone were to come to our village, our neighborhood, our place of work, and that person began to describe Jesus, would anybody hearing the description say, "We know Him well; He has been living here for years!"

Was that man's mission to embody Jesus' love really any different than our own? Can anyone who calls himself or herself a Christian seriously think Jesus offers exemptions to some of us from the need to imitate him? The man in the story knew Jesus' love had to shine through his actions. We must come to the same conclusion. The time and place and circumstances will be dif-

Can anyone who calls himself or herself a Christian seriously think Jesus offers exemptions to some of us from the need to imitate him?

ferent—but not the heart. And, if we're living as Jesus would, not the impact either. This kind of life *is possible*. It is not meant to be exceptional. It is the natural result of the supernatural work of Jesus in regular people who live each day training to be like him.

Be assured of one thing. No one ever drifts into this kind of full devotion. Daily pressures relentlessly pull us in the other direction. It takes resolve to engage in the practices, experiences, and relationships that draw us upward toward Christ and empower us to do what we cannot do by merely trying hard. But when pursued rightly and creatively, these practices are not burdensome. Rightly pursued, they lead us to that which God most wants us to experience—*life*. Free, vital, and fruitful "running-over" life.

Jesus invites you to seek this kind of life in his kingdom. *That* is the goal of true spirituality. Like the one "pearl of great value," it is infinitely worth pursuing.

Excerpt taken from *Windows of the Soul* by Ken Gire. Copyright 1986 by Ken Gire Jr. Used by permission of Zondervan Publishing House.

SPIRITUAL EXERCISE

Consider again the question Ken Gire poses:

I wonder. If someone were to come to our village, our neighborhood, our place of work, and that person began to describe Jesus, would anybody hearing the description say, "We know Him well; He has been living here for years!"

Take this question with you this week. Bring it to mind as you interact with family, friends, coworkers, neighbors, people in need, even perfect strangers.

As those around you observe your life, are they observing Jesus' life? How likely is it that they would say, "We know Him well," based on their knowledge of you?

BIBLE STUDY

1. <u>In Galatians 5:22–23</u>, Paul paints a picture of fruitful spiritual life. Read the passage and list each fruit below. Now write a brief definition or description after each. Consider actually consulting a dictionary.

love — treat others as (christian) brothers, do not judge
joy — an intense happiness
peace — let God take charge, and receive His comfort in all circumstances
patience — quietly seek God's will
kindness — seek what you can do for the needy, physically + give encouragement
goodness — treat others we seek to be treated
faithfulness — remain God's person despite bad situations
gentleness — be aware of others feelings, do not be pushy or vindictive
self-control — remember who you represent and act accordingly — Reconsider initial thoughts of doing something unwise when you are offended

2. Reflecting on your life over the past few months, which of the above fruits have been most evident?

Which have been least evident?

3. It is the goal of spiritual life "to know Jesus more intimately and live as if he were in your place." When you distill that goal to its essence—when you get down to the core of the core—you will always find love. Read 1 John 3:11–24. Summarize all of the ways that love finds expression as you imitate Christ.

16 – He laid down His life for us
17 – help brother in need
18 – love in deed and truth
followes our heart; have confidence before god

4. The most well-known love passage in the Bible is found in 1 Corinthians 13:1–13. Take a few moments to read the passage carefully. Note that in verses 4–7, you could replace the word "love" with the word "Jesus" and the passage would still be entirely true. Write down those verses below, inserting your name instead. (excellence of love)
1. speak well – w/o love, it's a noisy gong
2. have great faith; w/o love, we are nothing
3. feed the poor, accept bodily harm; w/o love, no profit
4. Jesus is patient, kind, free of jealousy, not arrogant is not selfish, does not get angry, is forgiving, never fails us, endures all things

As you reflect on the above, what does it tell you about your "love life" these days? Has your expression of love been increasing or declining? Why?

5. How deeply have you *felt* God's love in recent days?

To what do you attribute this?

6. Considering questions 1–5, what conclusions do you come to regarding the current health of your spiritual life?

Could improve

What, if any, changes do you see necessary?

7. Look back over the previous sessions. Pick out at least one highlight from each reading, exercise, or Bible study—a point or truth you want to be sure to remember—and list it below.

Session 1

Session 2

Session 3

Session 4

Session 5

Session 6

8. What issue would you like to study and discuss more—either for greater clarification or because you want to seal the matter in your heart and life?

9. What can fellow group members do to help you move forward in your spiritual journey?

What do you think you can do for each of them?

TAKE-AWAY

My summary of the main point of this session, and how it impacts me personally:

> NOTE: You will fill in this information after your group discussion. Leave it blank until the conclusion of your meeting.

Leader's Guide

How to Use This Discussion Guide

Doers of the Word

One of the reasons small groups are so effective is because when people are face-to-face, they can discuss and process information instead of merely listening passively. *God's truths are transforming* only to the extent they are received and absorbed. Just as uneaten food cannot nourish, truth "out there"—either in a book or spoken by a teacher—cannot make a difference if it is undigested. Even if it is bitten off and chewed, it must be swallowed and made part of each cell to truly give life.

The spiritual transformation at the heart of this Bible study series can occur only if people get truth and make that truth part of their lives. Reading about sit-ups leaves you flabby; doing sit-ups gives you strong abdominals. That's why in every session, we present group members exercises to do during the week. They also study Scripture on their own in (hopefully) unhurried settings where they can meditate on and ponder the truths that are encountered. Group discussion is the other way we've designed for them to grab hold of these important lessons.

This study is not a correspondence course. It's a personal and group experience designed to help believers find a biblical approach to their spiritual lives that really works. We recognize that people have a variety of learning styles, so we've tried to incorporate a variety of ways to learn. One of the most important ways they will learn is when they meet together to process the information verbally in a group.

Not Question-by-Question

One approach to learning used by some small groups encourages members to systematically discuss *everything* they learn on their own during the group time. Such material is designed so group members do a study and then report what their answers were for each question. While this approach is thorough, it can become boring. The method we've adopted includes individual study, but we do not suggest discussing *everything* in the session when you meet. Instead, questions are given to leaders (hence, this Leader's Guide) to get at the heart of the material without being rote recitations of the answers the members came up with on their own. This may be a bit confusing at first, because some people fill in the blanks, expecting each answer to be discussed, and discussed in the order they wrote them down. Instead, you, as a leader, will be asking questions *based* on their study, but not necessarily numerically corresponding to their study. We think this technique of handling the sessions has the best of both approaches: individual learning is reinforced in the group setting without becoming wearisome.

It is also important that you understand you will not be able to cover all the material provided each week. We give you more than you can use in every session—not to frustrate you, but to give you enough so you can pick and choose. *Base your session plan on the needs of individual members of your group.*

There may be a few times when the material is so relevant to your group members that every question seems to fit. Don't feel bad about taking two weeks on a session. The purpose of this series is transformational life-change, not timely book completion!

Getting Ready for *Your* Group

We suggest that to prepare for a meeting, you first do the study yourself and spend some time doing the spiritual exercise. Then look over the questions we've given you in the Leader's Guide. As you consider your group members and the amount of discussion time you have, ask yourself if the questions listed for that session relate to your group's needs. Would some other questions fit better? We've tried to highlight the main points of each session, but you may feel you need to hit some aspect harder than we did, or not spend as much time on a point. As long as your preparation is based on knowledge of your group, customize the session however you see fit.

As we pointed out, you may have to adapt the material because of time considerations. It is very hard to discuss every topic in a given session in detail—we certainly don't recommend it. You may also only have a limited time because of the nature of your group. Again, the purpose isn't to cover every question exhaustively, but to get the main point across in each session (whatever incidental discussion may otherwise occur). As a guide to your preparation, review the *Primary Focus* statement at the beginning and the *Session Highlights* paragraph at the end of each session's Leader's Guide. They represent our attempt to summarize what we were trying to get across in writing the sessions. If your questions get at those points, you're on the right track.

A Guide, Not a Guru

Now a word about your role as leader. We believe all small groups need a leader. While it is easy to see that a group discussion would get off track without a facilitator, we would like you to ponder another very important reason you hold the position you do.

This Bible study series is about spiritual growth—about Christ being formed in each of us. One of the greatest gifts you can give another person is to pay attention to his or her spiritual life. As a leader, you will serve your group members by observing their lives and trying to hear, in the questions they ask and the answers they give, where they are in their spiritual development. Your discerning observations are an invaluable contribution to their spiritual progress. That attention, prayer, and insight is an extremely rare gift—but it is revolutionary for those blessed enough to have such a person in their lives. You are that person. You give that gift. You can bring that blessing.

People desperately need clarity about spirituality. Someone needs to blow away the fog that surrounds the concept of what it means to live a spiritual life and give believers concrete ideas how to pursue it. Spiritual life is just *life*. It's that simple. Christ-followers must invite God into all aspects of life, even the everyday routines. That is where we spend most of our time anyway, so that is where we must be with God. If not, the Christian life will become pretense, or hypocrisy. We must decompartmentalize life so that we share it all with God in a barrier-free union with him.

We say all this so that you, the leader, can be encouraged in and focused on your role. You are the person observing how people are doing. You are the one who detects the doors people will not let God through, the one who sees the blind spots they don't, the one who gently points out the unending patience of God who will not stop working in us until "his work is completed" (Phil. 1:6). You will hold many secret conversations with God about the people in your group—while you meet, during a phone call, sitting across the table at lunch, when you're alone. In addition to making the meeting happen, this is one of the most important things you can do to be a catalyst for life-change. That is why you're meeting together anyway—to see people become more like Christ. If you lead as a *facilitator* of discussion, not a teacher, and a *listener* rather than the one who should be listened to, you will see great changes in the members of your group.

What Is True Spirituality?

Primary Focus: To understand that true spirituality is growing more and more intimate with Christ and living as if he were in your place.

Remember that these questions do not correspond numerically with the questions in the assignment. We do not recommend simply going over what your group members put for their answers—that will probably result in a tedious discussion at best. Rather, use some or all of these questions (and perhaps some of your own) to stimulate discussion; that way, you'll be processing the content of the session from a fresh perspective each meeting.

1. Reread the following quote from Dallas Willard's *The Spirit of the Disciplines* to your group members:

   How many people are radically and permanently repelled from The Way by Christians who are unfeeling, stiff, unapproachable, boringly lifeless, obsessive, and dissatisfied? Yet such Christians are everywhere, and what they are missing is the wholesome liveliness springing from a balanced vitality within the freedom of God's loving rule. . . . "Spirituality" wrongly understood or pursued is a major source of human misery and rebellion against God.

   What are some signs that indicate a person might be engaged in spirituality wrongly understood or pursued?

   NOTE: Group members' answers will probably include some of the following phrases. You may add to their comments from what is listed below:

   - Spiritual life separate from ordinary life
   - Artificial, human-made spirituality
   - Spiritual disciplines that become competitive activities

> • Amassing biblical knowledge without life-change
> • Ceasing certain bad habits and behaviors without inner transformation (examples: quitting swearing but continuing to gossip or shade truth; attending church meetings but not being loving toward non-Christian family members; saying "Praise the Lord" but living a joyless, superficial life)

2. *(Regarding question 4 in the Bible study)* In what ways have you ever fallen prey to spirituality wrongly understood and pursued? What was the by-product in your life?

3. What is your reaction to the definition of spirituality from the reading assignment? ("To pursue spiritual life means to know Jesus more intimately and live as if he were in your place.") How did your study of Scripture reinforce this definition?

4. *(Regarding question 7 in the Bible study)* What is *your* spiritual health like according to this definition?

5. What were your feelings about the spiritual exercise—was it easy, frustrating, joyful, confusing? Were there times when you got it right? How about times when you fell short? What did you learn through this experience?

6. What impact did your Bible study and reading assignments have on your experience of trying to live out your daily activities in Jesus' name?

7. Fill in the blank: "If there is one area in which I need to walk more like Jesus it's _____."

Take-Away: At the conclusion of your discussion each week, take a few minutes to have group members sum up the session and its impact on them by filling in the Take-Away section at the end of each session. Don't tell them what they are supposed to write—let them be true to their own experiences. When they have written their summaries, have everyone share with the others what they wrote. Statements should be similar to the statements in Session Highlights. If you feel the whole group may have missed an important aspect of the session, be sure to bring that up in the closing discussion.

Session Highlights: Spiritual life must not become rigid or compartmentalized; *all* of life is of interest and value to God; life according to Jesus' design is to know him more intimately and to live as he would if he were in my place.

Grace

Primary Focus: To understand how God's grace is the basis not just for forgiveness of sins, but for every aspect of life with him.

1. What was a highlight from your spiritual experiment to live a day conscious of God's grace?

2. In the parable of the prodigal son, a father had two sons. In what ways did *both* sons leave their father's side?

> NOTE: The one son left physically, which eventually led to regret and repentance; the other, though remaining in the father's vicinity, refused to have a meaningful relationship with the father—which led to bitterness and eventually jealously toward the brother who did.

3. *(Regarding question 2 in the Bible study)* What attracts you to leave the Father's house and live far away from him?

4. *(Regarding question 3 in the Bible study)* In what way are you sometimes like the dutiful, stay-at-home son?

5. *(Regarding question 5 in the Bible study)* In real life, parents have children for a variety of reasons. From your study of Scripture this week, what explains why your heavenly Father wanted *you* to be born?

6. Obviously, the father in the parable longs to be with his sons, and reuniting with his lost son gave him great pleasure. Listen to this quote from Henri Nouwen (read it to your group members):

   Wouldn't it be wonderful to make God smile by giving God the chance to find me and love me lavishly? ... Do I believe that there is a real desire in God to simply be with me?

   What is your reaction to this quote?

7. Review this quote from Nouwen (reread it to your group members):

For a long time I have lived with the insight that returning to my Father's home was the ultimate call. It has taken me much spiritual work to make the elder son as well as the younger son in me turn around and receive the welcoming love of the Father. The fact is that, on many levels, I am still returning. But the closer I come to home the clearer becomes the realization that there is a call beyond the call to return.... I now see that the hands that forgive, console, heal, and offer a festive meal must become my own.

What enables us to go from a position of feeling at home with the Father to taking on the job of extending grace toward other prodigals?

> NOTE: It requires effort to overcome the complacency that comes with feeling "at home" with the Father. Having said that, the more we know of God's grace, the more we should naturally want to invite others into it. If we're not experiencing grace, we will probably have limited enthusiasm about asking others to join us. If the goodness of God is our daily experience, the subsequent reflexive joy will spill over into conversations with others.

8. Why is it so important to feel at home with the Father if we want to live as if Jesus were in our place?

> NOTE: Jesus was clearly always at home with the Father; to imitate him, we must also be. Attempts to live like Jesus will fail if they are not based on the assurance of the Father's love and acceptance of us. The security and power of the Christian life comes from knowing how good God is, and in knowing we'll never find what we're looking for anywhere else but in the company and close fellowship of our heavenly Father.

Session Highlights: God is gracious toward me and wants me to live in, and extend, that grace every day.

> NOTE: The next session contains an extended solitude exercise in place of the usual Bible study and spiritual exercise. We suggest you alert your group to this so that they allow adequate time for this experience.

SESSION THREE

Growth

Primary Focus: To understand that spiritual growth is a process that happens by *training,* not just by *trying hard* to be like Jesus.

1. Although he certainly could, why do you think God doesn't zap us with instant spiritual maturity?

> NOTE: God always wants to treat us as creatures in his image. You can turn a board into a shelf, but personal transformation requires cooperation with the person—not raw power. God also wants a relationship built on trust, one that is intimate and meaningful; instant spiritual maturity would sabotage that process. God wants us to participate in our growth program as a way to affirm our dignity and allow for us to share in the gratification of what is accomplished.

2. What is the difference between a person *trying* to be like Jesus and a person *training* to be like Jesus?

3. In general terms, what negative reactions (if any) do you have to the concept of training? What do you think of spiritual training?

4. What training activities are working well for you right now? What aren't? What new activities might you like to try?

> NOTE: Take the remainder of the meeting time to debrief the solitude exercise that was done this week. Because of the length of that experience, give plenty of time for each group member to react to it.

5. Regarding your spiritual experiment this past week:

   How did it feel to engage in that extended time of solitude? What aspects of the experience were hard? Which came easy? What areas of growth did you note?

What is an area in which you still need growth?

What did you feel at the conclusion of your time? Do you think you'll do something like this again soon? Why or why not?

Session Highlights: Growth comes from training to be like Jesus—not simply trying to be like Jesus; we may have a variety of reactions to spiritual exercises, but they are indispensable tools for spiritual growth.

SESSION FOUR

Groups

Primary Focus: To understand the transforming power of relationships when they are vehicles for truth and grace.

1. Describe a time since the last meeting when you had to dispense *truth* in Jesus' name. Describe a time when you extended *grace*. How did these times turn out?

2. Describe how being in relationships that provide a balance of truth and grace can help you in the following areas:

   Guidance and decision-making
   Dealing with inner struggles
   Addressing character flaws
   Feeling forgiven
   Times of discouragement or grief

3. Which way does your view of God lean these days: is God more interested in truth-telling or grace-giving? What factors in your life account for the way you've been perceiving God?

4. *(Regarding question 3 of the Bible study)* What are you more naturally: a grace-giver or a truth-teller? How has this strength helped you over the years? What would be the benefit of finding a better balance between the two?

5. *(Regarding questions 4 and 5 in the Bible study)* Given your natural tendency, which scriptural truths do you need to bring continually to mind?

6. How good are you when it comes to receiving grace? What about receiving truth? In what ways can our small group help you accept these more readily?

7. *(Regarding question 6 in the Bible study)* What are some ways to express difficult truth graciously?

> NOTE: Here are some tangible examples of expressing difficult truth in gracious ways:
>
> - Start any confrontation by affirming the relationship.
> - Encourage the person for whatever is worthy of encouragement.
> - Avoid emotionally charged, accusatory statements or anything meant to irritate the person.
> - Don't use sarcasm; speak about your feelings directly.
> - Watch your tone of voice and volume.

8. *(Regarding question 8 in the Bible study)* How are we doing with grace and truth in our group?

Session Highlights: Relationships that help us live like Christ are characterized by grace-giving and truth-telling; we need to be aware of our natural tendencies and grow to extend a balance of truth and grace in God-honoring ways.

A Word about Leadership: Remember the comments at the beginning of this discussion guide about your role as a leader? About now, it's probably a good idea to remind yourself that one of your key functions is to be a cheerleader—someone who seeks out signs of spiritual progress in others and makes some noise about it!

What have you seen God doing in your group members' lives as a result of this study? Don't assume they've seen that progress—and definitely don't assume they are beyond needing simple words of encouragement. Find ways to point out to people the growth you've seen. Let them know it's happening, and that it's noticeable to you and others.

There aren't a whole lot of places in this world where people's spiritual progress is going to be recognized and celebrated. After all, wouldn't you like to hear someone cheer you on? So would your group members. You have the power to make a profound impact through a sincere, insightful remark.

Be aware, also, that some groups get sidetracked by a difficult member or situation that hasn't been confronted. And some individuals could be making significant progress—they just need a nudge. Encouragement is not about just saying nice things;

it's about offering *words that urge*. It's about giving courage (en-*courage*-ment) to those who lack it.

So, take a risk. Say what needs to be said to encourage your members toward their goal of becoming fully devoted followers.

Gifts

Primary Focus: To understand how we are transformed as we use our gifts in a Christlike life of servanthood.

1. Based on this week's exercise, what did you learn about yourself as you attempted to serve others? In what ways did you sense God's transforming work in you as you served? Were there any factors that kept you from serving as you would have liked to?

> NOTE: Be sure to take time for your group members to give thoughtful answers to this question; if they reflect honestly before answering, this question will generate profound personal insights. For example, people may have discovered God pointing out that they resist service, or they may have been encouraged by observing that serving others actually brought unexpected joy.

2. *(Regarding question 2 in the Bible study)* Which side of the continuum do you lean toward: the desire to be noticed or the desire to be unrecognized? What aspects of your personality, upbringing, etc. contribute to this tendency?

3. Other than Jesus, who is your personal hero when it comes to an example of servanthood? Why do you think that person has such a good handle on this character strength?

4. What has been one of your greatest joys in serving others? What is one of your greatest fears when it comes to living out a lifestyle of servanthood?

> NOTE: People often fear the results of a distorted kind of servanthood—they picture themselves being mistreated or forced to become a doormat for God. They also fear God will spoil their plans—that if they become more of a servant, it would radically redirect the course of their lives away from activities they enjoy.

5. *(Regarding question 7 in the Bible study)* In Philippians 2:1–11, Paul explained Jesus' commitment to servanthood and how God honors that commitment. How does Christ's example of setting aside his divine prerogatives—all the benefits and status he had in heaven—to become a lowly servant of others inspire you to become a servant? What are some other observations you can make about the teaching in that passage and our lives of service?

> NOTE: When Christ humbled himself on earth, his humility did not involve timidity, cringing, or self-loathing. Because of this proper view of servanthood, he was empowered to serve others fully and did not have to get something in return—there were no strings attached to his love. In addition, because of the glory which he knew would follow after the resurrection, he was able to endure his hardships. We, too, must take courage that this world's setbacks are not the final chapter, and great rewards await us even if, as we serve others in this life, we are misunderstood or unappreciated.

6. Where does spiritual giftedness come into play in this concept of a lifestyle of servanthood?

> NOTE: We must focus our servanthood consistent with our abilities and passions. We are all different; that's why more gets done when we all serve in harmony with who God made us to be and what he gifted us to do.
>
> Be sure that, as the leader, you are helping your group members identify what their next steps are for developing their gifts. (There are many helpful resources available. One that we recommend is a Groupware published by Zondervan called *Network*.) These steps will not be the same for everyone. This is one of those times when being a good shepherd means a one-size-fits-all approach won't work! Help each group member know what will make the most sense for his or her personal development.

Session Highlights: Living as Jesus lived means going beyond mere occasional helpfulness; it means voluntarily becoming a servant.

SESSION SIX

Giving

Primary Focus: To understand how the generous stewarding of our resources transforms our hearts.

1. What are some of the difficulties you have living as Jesus would in our intensely materialistic culture?

NOTE: Discuss problems such as:

- discontentment/always wanting more
- envy
- debt
- cold-heartedness toward those in need

---

2. What did you experience through the exercise? What are some specific ways you have seen God change your spending habits because you are a Christian? In what ways are you becoming aware of changes needed in this area?

3. *(Regarding question 1 in the Bible study)* What conclusions did you come to concerning the two parables? What lingering doubts keep you from believing that pursuing God's kingdom (instead of your own) is really worth it?

4. *(Regarding question 2 in the Bible study)* How would you summarize the attitudes and behaviors God asks of us regarding money and possessions?

5. Why do you think being a good steward sometimes seems like a dull or difficult way of life? What truth can you bring to bear on that common misunderstanding?

NOTE: Saying no to an impulsive purchase may leave you feeling temporarily empty. Don't kid yourself that years of bad habits will go away easily or painlessly. Only after time and

---

> practice will the rewards of good stewardship and a lifstyle of giving be felt.

6. *(Regarding question 3 in the Bible study)* Describe a time when you were a cheerful, generous giver. What prompted that lavish act? In what ways did you experience the promises Paul described?

7. *(Regarding question 5 in the Bible study)* How do Jesus' words help you assess what you are valuing these days? What steps might you need to take to get out of your comfort zone and live more compassionately?

> NOTE: This might be a good time for your group to do some kind of extension project together to serve those in need. As you prepare for this meeting, come up with a few ideas of what you could do as a group. Your church or other local ministries might be able to provide you with suggestions — or your group may know of an individual or family in need. Discuss with your group members what activity you might undertake to put your learning into action.

8. *(Regarding question 6 in the Bible study)* How did you summarize what it means to "seek first [God's] kingdom and his righteousness" — especially as it pertains to our material resources?

9. *(Regarding question 7 in the Bible study)* What would it take for you to entrust your treasures to God in the way described?

Session Highlights: We are treasuring creatures; what we treasure not only reveals our hearts, but shapes them as well; our hearts are shaped away from possessiveness and greed as we cultivate a lifestyle of giving; Jesus' priority of treasuring people must become ours; although it may seem at first like a difficult or dreary challenge, the life Jesus offers is so much better than anything the world ever could.

SESSION SEVEN

"We Know Him Well . . ."

Primary Focus: To be reminded that the goal of spiritual life is to live in such a way that others say, "We know Him well. . . ."

1. What was your reaction to the story of the missionary in the reading? In what ways was it hard to identify with that man's life? In what ways could you envision yourself having a similar impact?

2. How did the spiritual exercise go this week? Did you find yourself living any differently because of Ken Gire's question?

3. *(Regarding questions 1 – 6 in the Bible study)* As you reflected on the fruit of the Spirit and on your ability to give and receive love, what did you observe? What conclusions did you come to regarding the current health of your spiritual life?

4. *(Regarding question 6 in the Bible study)* What changes, if any, do you need to make in the way you are pursuing your spiritual life? Speaking practically, what will that take?

5. What are some of the highlights you noted from the past sessions in this study?

> NOTE: Take plenty of time on this question. Hopefully everyone will have several highlights to share.

6. What can this group do to help you move forward in your spiritual journey?

7. How have your original expectations been met (or not met) during the course of this study?

Session Highlights: The goal of spiritual living is no more complicated than to know Jesus more intimately and live as he would if he were in my place; that kind of life will make a profound impact on the people around me; it is also the only life worth living, full of meaning and joy.

John C. Ortberg Jr. is teaching pastor at Willow Creek Community Church in South Barrington, Illinois. He is the author of *The Life You've Always Wanted* and *Love Beyond Reason*. John and his wife, Nancy, live in the Chicago area with their three children, Laura, Mallory, and Johnny.

Laurie Pederson, a real estate investment manager, is a founding member of Willow Creek Community Church. As an elder since 1978, she has helped shape many of the foundational values and guiding principles of the church. She is cocreator of Willow Creek's discipleship-based church membership process. Laurie lives outside of Chicago with her husband, Scott.

Judson Poling, a staff member at Willow Creek Community Church since 1980, writes small group training materials and many of the dramas performed in Willow Creek's outreach services. He is coauthor of the *Walking with God* and *Tough Questions* Bible study series and general editor of *The Journey: A Study Bible for Spiritual Seekers*. He lives in Algonquin, Illinois, with his wife, Deb, and their two children, Anna and Ryan.

Willow Creek Association

Vision, Training, Resources for Prevailing Churches

This resource was created to serve you and to help you build a local church that prevails. It is just one of many ministry tools that are part of the Willow Creek Resources® line, published by the Willow Creek Association together with Zondervan.

The Willow Creek Association (WCA) was created in 1992 to serve a rapidly growing number of churches from across the denominational spectrum that are committed to helping unchurched people become fully devoted followers of Christ. Membership in the WCA now numbers over 10,000 Member Churches worldwide from more than ninety denominations.

The Willow Creek Association links like-minded Christian leaders with each other and with strategic vision, training, and resources in order to help them build prevailing churches designed to reach their redemptive potential. Here are some of the ways the WCA does that.

- **Prevailing Church Conference**—an annual two-and-a-half day event, held at Willow Creek Community Church in South Barrington, Illinois, to help pioneering church leaders raise up a volunteer core while discovering new and innovative ways to build prevailing churches that reach unchurched people.

- **Leadership Summit**—a once-a-year, two-and-a-half-day conference to envision and equip Christians with leadership gifts and responsibilities. Presented live at Willow Creek as well as via satellite broadcast to over sixty locations across North America, this event is designed to increase the leadership effectiveness of pastors, ministry staff, volunteer church leaders, and Christians in the marketplace.

- **Ministry-Specific Conferences**—throughout each year the WCA hosts a variety of conferences and training events—both at Willow Creek's main campus and off-site, across the U.S. and around the world—targeting church leaders in ministry-specific areas such as: evangelism, the arts, children, students, small groups, preaching and teaching, spiritual formation, spiritual gifts, raising up resources, etc.

- **Willow Creek Resources®**—to provide churches with trusted and field-tested ministry resources in such areas as leadership, evangelism, spiritual formation, spiritual gifts, small groups, stewardship, student ministry, children's ministry, the use of the arts—drama, media, contemporary music—and more. For additional information about Willow Creek Resources® call the Customer Service Center at 800-570-9812. Outside the U.S. call 847-765-0070.

- *WillowNet*—the WCA's Internet resource service, which provides access to hundreds of transcripts of Willow Creek messages, drama scripts, songs, videos, and multimedia tools. The system allows users to sort through these elements and download them for a fee. Visit us online at www.willowcreek.com.

- *WCA News*—a quarterly publication to inform you of the latest trends, resources, and information on WCA events from around the world.

- *Defining Moments*—a monthly audio journal for church leaders featuring Bill Hybels and other Christian leaders discussing probing issues to help you discover biblical principles and transferable strategies to maximize your church's redemptive potential.

- *The Exchange*—our online classified ads service to assist churches in recruiting key staff for ministry positions.

- **Member Benefits**—includes substantial discounts to WCA training events, a 20 percent discount on all Willow Creek Resources®, access to a Members-Only section on WillowNet, monthly communications, and more. Member Churches also receive special discounts and premier services through WCA's growing number of ministry partners—Select Service Providers.

For specific information about WCA membership, upcoming conferences, and other ministry services contact:

Willow Creek Association
P.O. Box 3188, Barrington, IL 60011-3188
Phone: 847-570-9812
Fax: 847-765-5046
www.willowcreek.com

a place where ...

nobody stands alone

Small groups, when they're working right, provide a place where you can experience continuous growth and community—the deepest level of community, modeled after the church in Acts 2, where believers are devoted to Christ's teachings and to fellowship with each other.

If you'd like to take the next step in building that kind of small group environment for yourself or for your church, we'd like to help.

The Willow Creek Association in South Barrington, Illinois, hosts an annual Small Groups Conference attended by thousands of church and small group leaders from around the world. Each year we also lead small group training events and workshops in seven additional cities across the country. We offer a number of small group resources for both small groups and small group leaders available to you through your local bookstore and Willow Creek Resources.

If you'd like to learn more, contact the Willow Creek Association at 1-800-570-9812. Or visit us on-line: www.willowcreek.com.